Incline My Heart

The Daily Search for Wondrous Things

Volume 2

Jason Hardin

DeWard
for your journey

Incline My Heart: The Daily Search for Wondrous Things (Vol. 2)
© 2024 by DeWard Publishing Company, Ltd.
P.O. Box 290696, Tampa, FL 33687
www.deward.com

Cover by nvoke design.

Printed in the United States of America.

ISBN: 978-1-947929-29-6

For Emma.

Last piece to our Party of 5 puzzle.
I love seeing the world through your eyes (and camera lens).

May the simple reflections in this little book
incline your beautiful heart toward home.

TABLE OF CONTENTS

Week Four

Week Five

Week Six

Week Seven

Week Eight

Week Nine

Week Ten

Week Eleven

Week Twelve

Week Thirteen

Preface

Your heart has immeasurable value. No earthly thing—no house, no vehicle, no vacation, no job, no degree, no amount of money, no retirement package—not one earthly thing matters more in the grand scheme of things than the condition of your God-given heart. You could spend the rest of your time on earth plumbing the depths of what your Creator has said about the human heart, and you won't hit the bottom of what there is to learn.

Your heart is the epicenter of trust and understanding, which is why Solomon encouraged in Proverbs 3.5–6:

> Trust in the LORD with all your heart,
>   and do not lean on your own understanding.
> In all your ways acknowledge him,
>   and he will make straight your paths.

Your heart is vulnerable to deception and distraction, which is why Solomon continued to wisely counsel in Proverbs 4.23:

> Keep your heart with all vigilance,
>   for from it flow the springs of life.

That sort of encouragement and counsel fills the pages of God's written revelation to mankind. He has spoken and inspired and preserved words for many, many reasons, but here's a big one: your heart was designed to incline. Like branches of a tree blown by the wind, our hearts can be bent, leaned, and bowed. Your heart *will* be inclined by the words you hear, believe, apply, and trust. Whether for good or ill depends on the source and truth of the words, which is why Solomon prefaced his proverbs with an invitation and a promise:

> My son, if you receive my words
>> and treasure up my commandments with you,
> making your ear attentive to wisdom
>> and **inclining your heart** to understanding;
> yes, if you call out for insight
>> and raise your voice for understanding,
> if you seek it like silver
>> and search for it as for hidden treasures,
> then you will understand the fear of the LORD
>> and find the knowledge of God. (Prov 2.1–5)

Since 2008, I've been jotting down simple reflections on my daily Bible readings. I've tried to keep them brief, heartfelt, and practical in hopes that they might be of some encouragement to my daughters in the years to come. I never really had any intention of publishing them in books, but as the collection has grown (and I've arrived at that point in my life where I'm thinking more and more about what I can leave behind as a blessing to others), this series of devotionals has grown to feel like a real contribution I can make. More often than not, I've written with my daughters in mind and, if the Lord wills, their eventual children and grandchildren. The process has been an immeasurable blessing to me. Perhaps the fruit of the process will be a blessing to you as well.

As I mentioned in Volume 1 of this series, I've found praying Psalm 119.18 to be helpful any time I open God's word—"Open my eyes, that I may behold wondrous things out of your law"—which is why we've called this series *The Daily Search for Wondrous Things*. But there is a goal for the beholding greater than idle notice, which is why Psalm 119.36 is also a great thing to pray.

Incline my heart to your testimonies,
    and not to selfish gain!

"Open my eyes and incline my heart." Our hearts will naturally bend toward the things that fill our eyes and minds. If your heart has immeasurable value, if it's been given to you by a perfect Creator who is good and does good, and if you are ultimately accountable to him, why *wouldn't* you humbly ask him to incline your heart toward him?

The approach of this devotional series is slightly different than your typical big book of 365 readings, one for each day of the year. There are no calendar dates, just weekday names (Sunday, Monday, etc.), which means these little books can be picked up and started at any point throughout the year. The readings flow each week in a simple pattern:

- **Sundays:** a reflection from the Psalms
- **Mondays, Wednesdays, and Fridays:** reflections from the Old Testament
- **Tuesdays, Thursdays, and Saturdays:** reflections from the New Testament

As the apostle Paul drew near to the conclusion of his letter to the Philippians, he wrote:

Finally, brothers, whatever is true, whatever is honorable, whatever is just, whatever is pure, whatever is lovely, whatever is commendable, if there is any excellence, if there is anything worthy of praise, think about these things. What you have learned and received and heard and seen in me—practice these things, and the God of peace will be with you. (Phil 4.8–9)

"Open and fill my eyes with truth, honor, justice, purity, loveliness, and excellence. Incline my heart towards what is truly commendable and worthy of praise. Help me see and appreciate your heart that I might become more like you." That's a wondrous thing to pray.

May these simple reflections incline your heart toward heaven and provide you a little more fuel for the journey. Most of all, may we walk with Jesus each and every day, every step of the way.

In his footsteps, the best is always yet to come.

See **https://www.ingodsimage.com/devotional-scripture-index/** for a Scripture index of this book and *Open My Eyes*, the first volume of the series.

WEEK ONE

SUNDAY

Wondrous Things

"Wondrous." Would you slow down long enough to think about that word with me for just a moment?

"Wondrous." It's one of those words we stretch for when words seem inadequate to describe what we're seeing or experiencing. "Wondrous" things are remarkable—worthy of undivided attention. "Wondrous" things are extraordinary—not to be glossed over or taken for granted. "Wondrous" things make us marvel; they amaze and even stun us at times. "Wondrous" things awaken that sacred sense of childlike curiosity within our sleepy hearts. In a world where "awesome" gets tossed around to describe everything from the Grand Canyon to pepperoni pizza, "wondrous" things are "awesome" things in every sense of the word.

You'll see all sorts of things today, and a great many of them won't be what you would have chosen if you could. Sad things. Scary things. Confusing things. Foolish things. Disheartening things. Worrisome things. Selfish things. Discouraging things. Hurtful things. Evil things. We all know we can't snap our fingers and make those things disappear, so what will we do?

Many of us will walk through the day aimlessly. We'll bounce off whatever circumstances surround us, just doing whatever we have to do to get through a day full of all those rough things. We'll be a lot like that "wave of the sea that is driven and tossed by the wind" (James 1.6). The eyes of our hearts will be closed and all we'll "see" is the good, the bad, and the ugly this world has to offer.

But what if we took the time to pray from hearts that are hungry and thirsty for "wondrous" things? What if we followed the lead of the psalmist and spoke directly to the God who hears...

Open my eyes, that I may behold
wondrous things out of your law. (Psa 119.18)

Make me understand the way of your precepts,
and I will meditate on your **wondrous** works. (Psa 119.27)

"Wondrous." You'll see all sorts of things today, and a great many of them won't be what you would have chosen if you could, but "wondrous" things are not beyond your reach. Our glorious God specializes in "wondrous" things. He has preserved an incredible revelation of "wondrous" works. He continues to invite us in to "wondrous" prayer. Every single day, his creation is full of "wondrous" testimony to his eternal power and divine nature.

It's so very easy to walk through a day, a week, a season, an entire lifetime blind, numb, and dulled to the "wondrous" because our minds are flooded with and anchored to so many earth-bound, temporary, trivial things. But if we would hear and feel and follow the prompt of Psalm 119 today...

Open my eyes...
Make me understand...

Clearly, we need "wondrous" help. We don't have it all together. We aren't sufficient in or of ourselves. But if we will slow down, tune out, log off... If we will take the time to seek the face of a truly "wondrous" God...

Open my eyes, that I may behold...
Make me understand, and I will meditate...

...we will discover all over again a deep, living well of "wondrous" things.

MONDAY

The Verbs on Page 1 Matter

In the beginning…

In the beginning, God was. God acted. Eight different verbs are used to describe for all time what God did "in the beginning." They are verbs worth thinking about today.

God **"created."** This universe isn't an accident, and neither are you. We're not living within a coincidence or blind fate or a meaningless void. We have a Maker.

God **"said."** Our Maker has not been silent. Not only has he expressed his intentions for his creation, he's preserved the revelation of those intentions for us. You can pick that revelation up and read it for yourself today—the Bible. God has spoken and you can know what he has said.

God **"saw."** Our Creator is not absent, distant, uninterested, or uninvolved. He sees. He knows.

God **"separated."** So much of his work has been "separating" work—light from darkness, the holy from the common, sin from himself, and those created in his image from sin.

God **"called."** From Page 1 of the Bible, he is the great Definer—day and night, male and female, good, very good, not good, and evil.

God **"made."** As a potter exercises sovereignty over a lump of clay, God has every right to express the meaning and purpose of his creation.

God **"set."** He has measured the waters in the hollow of his hand, marked off the heavens with a span, and weighed the mountains in scales. He is the establisher of limits, periods, and boundaries.

God **"blessed"**—a precious verb that reveals his deepest desire for humanity.

> "He made from one man every nation of mankind to live on all the face of the earth, having determined allotted periods and the boundaries of their dwelling place, that they should seek God, and perhaps feel their way toward him and find him. Yet he is actually not far from each one of us, for 'In him we live and move and have our being.'" (Acts 17.26–28)

God **created, said, saw, separated, called, made, set,** and **blessed**. He wants what is best for his creation.

When we ignore the verbs of Genesis 1, not only are we missing out on the best, we—the created—are "without excuse" (Rom 1.20). Romans 1 goes on to strongly warn that when we fail to honor him as God or give thanks to him, we become futile in our thinking, and our foolish hearts are darkened.

The verbs on Page 1 of your Bible matter. Carry them with you today. Allow them to shape your thinking and cast light on your path. They have been preserved to introduce us to the greatest reality in the universe.

TUESDAY

Herod Died. Jesus Lives.

Now after Jesus was born in Bethlehem of Judea in the days of Herod the king, behold, wise men from the east came to Jerusalem, saying, "Where is he who has been born king of the Jews? For we saw his star when it rose and have come to worship him." When Herod the king heard this, he was troubled, and all Jerusalem with him... (Matt 2.1–3)

Herod the king wasn't Herod the invincible or Herod the inevitable. He may have seemed like it at times. "The days of Herod the king" were unimaginably tough for many who lived through them. Evil could be seen and felt. Selfishness and greed wrought havoc on the innocent. But Herod the king was Herod the finite.

He could **scheme**.

...assembling all the chief priests and scribes of the people, he inquired of them where the Christ was to be born. (2.4)

He could **lie**.

"Go and search diligently for the child, and when you have found him, bring me word, that I too may come and worship him." (2.8)

He could **rage**.

Then Herod, when he saw that he had been tricked by the wise men, became furious... (2.16)

He could **murder**.

…he sent and killed all the male children in Bethlehem and in all that region who were two years old or under… (2.16)

He could **unleash terrible heartache**.

"A voice was heard in Ramah,
     weeping and loud lamentation,
Rachel weeping for her children;
     she refused to be comforted, because they are no more." (2.18)

But Herod the finite couldn't keep God's plan from coming to fruition.

Jesus was born "in the days of Herod the king" because the Almighty deemed it "the right time" (Rom 5.6). More than 700 years before Herod was born, the prophet Micah had foretold…

"And you, O Bethlehem, in the land of Judah,
     are by no means least among the rulers of Judah;
for from you shall come a ruler
     who will shepherd my people Israel." (2.6)

…and there wasn't one thing Herod the finite could do to prevent it.

As hard as it would have been to see in those dark days, Herod was limited. Herod the king was Herod the temporary. Joseph, Mary, and the child "departed to Egypt and remained there *until the death of Herod*" (2.14–15). Matthew 2.19–20 puts it bluntly:

But *when Herod died*, behold, an angel of the Lord appeared in a dream to Joseph in Egypt, saying, "Rise, take the child and his mother and go to the land of Israel, for those who sought the child's life are dead."

Evil is real. It's on heartbreaking display throughout Matthew 2. Some days, it seems like it's everywhere. Some nights, it can be felt. Some seasons, it's easy to wonder whether evil won't eventually swallow everything up in terrible triumph.

But Matthew 2 is also a timeless reminder that the shadows are temporary. The "Herods" of this world continue to rage, yielding their hearts and lending their power to the spiritual forces of evil…

…for a little while. They are not invincible. They are not inevitable. Darkness in the present will not have the definitive last word.

Wickedness is, but will not be forever.

The darkness has already done its worst. The Son has risen.

The kingdoms of earth pass away one by one. The kingdom of heaven remains.

Herod died. Jesus lives.

WEDNESDAY

Ezras Still Need Shecaniahs

"Ezra." If you're familiar with the Old Testament of the Bible, you remember the name. "Shecaniah"? Probably not. But here's something we all need to understand: the "Ezras" of the world desperately need the "Shecaniahs."

In Ezra 10, after rebuilding the temple, restoring the Passover, and contending with a wide variety of adversaries, Ezra was worn out and discouraged. The people were distracted and dangerously close to slipping into the old patterns of behavior that had led to the exile of their forefathers. And Ezra had reached the end of his rope.

> While Ezra prayed and made confession, weeping and casting himself down before the house of God, a very great assembly of men, women, and children gathered to him out of Israel, for the people wept bitterly. And Shecaniah the son of Jehiel, of the sons of Elam, addressed Ezra: "We have broken faith with our God and have married foreign women from the peoples of the land, but even now there is hope for Israel in spite of this. Therefore let us make a covenant with our God to put away all these wives and their children, according to the counsel of my lord and of those who tremble at the commandment of our God, and let it be done according to the Law. Arise, for it is your task, and we are with you; be strong and do it." (10.1–4)

Ezra has a book of the Bible named after him. Shecaniah doesn't. Ezra was known by Artaxerxes, king of Persia. Shecaniah wasn't. Ezra is remembered for standing before a great assembly of people, reading the Book of the Law of Moses for hours, and leading a multitude to repentance and restoration. Shecaniah isn't. But Ezra 10 documents a dark day. A deep valley. Ezra was bitterly weeping, with tear-streamed face to the ground. And Shecaniah was there to help.

Shecaniah was honest about the current predicament. He didn't gloss over the mess. He didn't downplay the seriousness of the situation. He didn't point fingers. He didn't cast the blame as far away from himself as he could. Notice the pronouns. "We have broken faith with our God."

He shared the gift of optimism and perspective with Ezra. "Even now there is hope."

He challenged Ezra. "Arise."

He reminded Ezra. "It is your task."

He strengthened Ezra with the blessing of fellowship. "We are with you."

He inspired Ezra. "Be strong and do it."

Then Ezra arose and Israel was motivated to take the next right step.

Your name might not be known by the masses. Your reputation may not open the doors of power. Your biography probably won't be written. But you *can* make a real difference today by following in Shecaniah's footsteps. Just look around. Who is worn out? Spent in the service of others? Maybe a little discouraged? Close to the end of their rope?

How could you serve as a refreshment to their souls?

Optimism. Perspective. Encouragement. A reminder. Strength. Fellowship. Inspiration. Those are the gifts Shecaniah gave on that tough day in Ezra 10.

In a darkened world full of discouragement, self-centeredness, and pessimism, be a Shecaniah this week.

THURSDAY

Sails Set in the Right Direction

In Acts 27, the apostle Paul and 275 other people were on a ship bound for Italy. The winds had recently been against them. Luke documents,

> We sailed slowly for a number of days and arrived with difficulty off Cnidus, and as the wind did not allow us to go farther, we sailed under the lee of Crete off Salmone. Coasting along it with difficulty, we came to a place called Fair Havens, near which was the city of Lasea. (27.7–8)

It had already been a strenuous journey and now, a decision had to be made—spend the winter in an unsuitable harbor or sail on into increasingly treacherous conditions.

> Since much time had passed, and the voyage was now dangerous because even the Fast was already over, Paul advised them, saying, "Sirs, I perceive that the voyage will be with injury and much loss, not only of the cargo and the ship, but also of our lives." But the centurion paid more attention to the pilot and to the owner of the ship than to what Paul said. (27.9–11)

It's that last sentence I'd encourage you to think about today. The Roman centurion had a choice to make in Fair Havens: listen to the pilot and owner of the ship or listen to a prisoner named Paul. He decided to "pay more attention" to the pilot and the ship's owner and by the end of the chapter, the ship was wrecked.

That literal shipwreck brings to mind Paul's first letter to Timothy and a much more serious shipwreck.

> This charge I entrust to you, Timothy, my child, in accordance with the prophecies previously made about you, that by them you may wage the good warfare, holding faith and a good conscience. By rejecting this, some have made shipwreck of their faith, among whom are Hymenaeus and Alexander... (1 Tim 1.18–19)

The circumstances between Acts 27 and 1 Timothy 1 were different, but shipwreck was the result in both situations because the right input was rejected.

Throughout 1 Timothy 1, Paul is warning young Timothy about difficult winds—different doctrines, myths which promote speculations rather than faithful stewardship, vain discussions, and confident assertions that swerve hearts into perilous territory. And in the middle of that metaphorical storm, Paul shows Timothy the anchor.

> The aim of our charge is love that issues from a pure heart and a good conscience and a sincere faith. (1.5)

This was the charge Paul was entrusting to Timothy. Grab on to the ropes of sincere faith and don't let go. Keep your heart pure and your conscience clean. Set your compass on love. Process the input and advice that comes your way with wisdom. Take care who you allow to steer the rudder of your life.

In Acts 27, the man in charge paid more attention to the pilot and owner of the ship than to what Paul said, and the ship wrecked. In 1 Timothy 1, two men paid more attention to what they wanted than to what Paul said, and the ship of their faith wrecked. Thousands of years later, difficult winds continue to blow and storms still pop up on the horizon. Paul lived a long time ago, but the lighthouse of "the gospel of the glory of the blessed God" with which he was entrusted is shining brightly today.

The world around you is filled with confusing, contrary voices anxious to steer you in conflicting, deadly directions. Come what may, remember: God is the owner of the vessel. Jesus is the most qualified pilot you could ask for. Grab on to the ropes of sincere faith and don't let go. Keep your heart pure and your conscience clean. Set your compass on love and the winds may blow in your face at times, but your sails will be set in the right direction.

FRIDAY

Overtaken By Blessings

"What does God want from me?" That's one of the biggest, most important questions any of us could ever ask. "What's he looking for? As the Provider of my time, my health, my daily resources and blessings, how can I live this week in a way that makes him proud? What does my Creator want me to be?"

Deuteronomy 28 contains three answers to those really big questions. Moses is giving his final instructions and reminders to the children of Israel, but the principles preserved for our learning are priceless and just as relevant as ever.

God wants me to fear his glorious and awesome name (28.58). He is the Lord. Yahweh. I AM. He has always been. He is Almighty. Divine. Holy. All-present. Eternally powerful. Infinitely wise. He's God, I'm not. Therefore, I ought to respect and honor his glorious, awesome name. But what will that *look* like?

God wants me to faithfully obey his voice, being careful to do what he says (28.1). As high as the heavens are above the earth, his ways are higher than our ways and his thoughts higher than our thoughts. His laws are perfect, reviving our souls. His testimonies are sure, making us wise. His precepts are right, causing our hearts to rejoice. His commandments are pure, enlightening our eyes. His rules are true and righteous altogether. He wants me to trust him. Obey him. *Why?*

Because this—fearing and obeying him—is the path to "joyfulness and gladness of heart"(28.47). My Creator wants the best for me, and what *is* the best? The path of life. He's made it known and he expects me to follow it. What's the best? Fullness of joy in his presence. Pleasures forevermore at his right hand. Gladness of heart. Abundant life. He's making it all known and asking me to trust him.

> "And all these blessings shall come upon you and overtake you, if you obey the voice of the LORD your God." (28.2)

Overtaken. What a potent, thought-provoking word! God wants you to be "**overtaken.**" Not by sin or selfishness. Not by evil or heartache. **Overtaken by blessings.** "If…" The choice is ours. Mine. Yours. Today.

Honor him. Obey him. Serve him with joyfulness and gladness of heart. Trust that he knows better and provides the best.

That's what our Creator wants from us and for us.

SATURDAY

1 Corinthians 13 Made Personal

> Love is patient and kind; love does not envy or boast; it is not arrogant or rude. It does not insist on its own way; it is not irritable or resentful; it does not rejoice at wrongdoing, but rejoices with the truth. Love bears all things, believes all things, hopes all things, endures all things. (1 Cor 13.4–7)

It's not hard to make that paragraph personal, just replace the word *love* with your name. Easy to do, but really convicting. Here's what it looks like for me:

> Jason is patient and kind; Jason does not envy or boast; Jason is not arrogant or rude. Jason does not insist on his own way; Jason is not irritable or resentful; Jason does not rejoice at wrongdoing, but rejoices with the truth. Jason bears all things, believes all things, hopes all things, endures all things.

Could I encourage you to take the time to do the same? Maybe read this next paragraph out loud, inserting your own name in the blanks below…

> _____ is patient and kind; _____ does not envy or boast; _____ is not arrogant or rude. _____ does not insist on his (or her) own way; _____ is not irritable or resentful; _____ does not rejoice at wrongdoing, but rejoices with the truth. _____ bears all things, believes all things, hopes all things, endures all things.

Looking at 1 Corinthians 13 from *that* angle, Jason is very much a work-in-progress. I'm guessing you're in the same boat. There are days that plugging my name into that paragraph is a little like trying to shove a square peg into a round hole. I'm thankful God isn't through with me yet. But I'm also thankful for the name that fits perfectly in 1 Corinthians 13.

> Jesus is patient and kind; Jesus does not envy or boast; Jesus is not arrogant or rude. Jesus does not insist on his own way; Jesus is not irritable or resentful; Jesus does not rejoice at wrongdoing, but rejoices with the truth. Jesus bears all things, believes all things, hopes all things, endures all things. Jesus never ends.

Learning from him, walking with him, and conforming myself to him is the greatest goal anyone can have—a goal worth taking seriously and making personal.

Patience. Kindness. Not envying or boasting. Not arrogant or rude. Not insisting on my own way. Not irritable, resentful, or rejoicing at wrongdoing. Rather, rejoicing in and with the truth. Bearing, believing, hoping, and enduring. That's Jesus. That's the path. That's the light this world needs—the light I want to reflect this weekend. How about you?

WEEK TWO

SUNDAY

Not Many, But There Is One

To how many kings of the world can you say, "Give attention to the sound of my cry"? How many "lords" were willing to hear your voice this morning? Maybe you enjoy something I don't, but there is a giant chasm between *my* words and the attention of those in the highest positions of power. I can't stroll into the Oval Office or the Senate Chamber or Buckingham Palace and say, "Give ear to my words."

But then I read Psalm 5, I hear David talk about "my King and my God," and my perspective is dramatically broadened. Just listen to the first three verses and marvel at what is being described.

> Give ear to my words, O Lord;
>> consider my groaning.
> Give attention to the sound of my cry,
>> my King and my God,
>> for to you do I pray.
> O Lord, in the morning you hear my voice;
>> in the morning I direct my prayer to you and watch.

To how many kings can I say, "Give attention to the sound of my cry"? Not many. Just one, really. But he's the greatest, the wisest, most powerful King of all, and he's "my King."

How many lords were willing to hear my voice this morning? Not many. Just one, in fact. But he's the most compassionate, patient, merciful, gracious Lord of all. He considers my groaning. He hears my voice, he cares about my prayers, and he *wants* to be known as "my God."

He's always been. He is, everywhere. He always will be. He's not a God who delights in wickedness; evil may not dwell with him (5.4). The boastful won't be able to defy him (5.5). Neither the evildoers, nor liars, nor the bloodthirsty will be able to escape him (5.5–6). I am completely unworthy of an audience with him, but through the abundance of his steadfast love, I can enter and bow in reverence before his holy presence (5.7). "Lead me," I'm invited and empowered to pray, "in your righteousness" (5.8).

Though I live for a little while in a world where truth is scarce, transgressions are abundant, and rebellion is leading many to destruction (5.9–10), "my King and my God" provides refuge. In that refuge is joy. Those of us who abide in this shelter of the Almighty "ever sing for joy" (5.11).

> For you bless the righteous, O LORD;
> you cover him with favor as with a shield. (5.12)

Who opens the door, walks into the bedroom of a king, and dares to ask for attention? Who can groan, cry out, or hope to just spend time in such regal quarters? Who knows they will not only be welcomed, but "covered with favor," night or day, because of their place in the heart of the king? Only sons and daughters of the king.

I'm guessing you're like me. There's a giant chasm between *your* words and the attention of those in the highest positions of power. Allow Psalm 5 to remind you. There aren't many movers and shakers who will consider, give attention to, or even hear you today. But there *is* one. The One. My King. Our God. Your Father in heaven.

> Give ear to my words, O LORD;
> consider my groaning.

Give attention to the sound of my cry,
     my King and my God,
     for to you do I pray.

What an indescribably precious gift...

MONDAY

Sunday's Song, Monday's Strength

In Nehemiah 8, as Ezra the scribe read the Book of the Law of Moses before a great assembly in Jerusalem, the people were reverent and attentive. As early morning progressed to midday, they were humbled and heartbroken by what they were hearing. Their generation was living in and rebuilding amidst the consequences of ignoring and rebelling against the Lord, the great God. "All the people wept as they heard the words of the Law" (8.9).

But before the assembly dispersed, Nehemiah and Ezra wanted the people to hear something loud and clear:

> "This day is holy to the Lord your God; do not mourn or weep… Go your way. Eat the fat and drink sweet wine and send portions to anyone who has nothing ready, for this day is holy to our Lord. And do not be grieved, for the joy of the Lord is your strength." (8.9–10)

In our assemblies yesterday, we sang some powerful, encouraging, perspective-shaping anthems.

God is so good. Jesus is real. He saved my soul. I praise his name.

…and today, the joy of the Lord is our strength. Yesterday we sang…

> Closing my eyes at eve and thinking of Heaven's grace,
>   Longing to see my Lord, yes, meeting Him face to face;

Trusting Him as my all wheresoever my footsteps roam,
    Pleading with Him to guide me on to the spirits' home!

Thomas R. Sweatman (1917)

...and today, the joy of the LORD is our strength. Yesterday we sang...

Were the whole realm of nature mine,
    That were a present far too small;
Love so amazing, so divine,
    Demands my soul, my life, my all!

Isaac Watts (1707)

...and today, the joy of the LORD is our strength. Yesterday we sang...

I'm pressing on the upward way,
    New heights I'm gaining every day;
Still praying as I onward bound,
    "Lord, plant my feet on higher ground."

Johnson Oatman, Jr. (1892)

...and today, the joy of the LORD is our strength. Yesterday we sang...

My sin—O the bliss of this glorious tho't!—
    My sin, not in part but the whole,
Is nailed to the cross, and I bear it no more.
    Praise the Lord, praise the Lord, O my soul!

Horatio G. Spafford (1873)

...and today, the joy of the LORD is our strength. Yesterday we sang...

The kingdoms of earth pass away one by one,
    But the kingdom of heaven remains;

It is built on a rock and the Lord is its King,
  And forever and ever He reigns.

Henry R. Trickett (1887)

...and today, the joy of the Lord is our strength. Yesterday we sang...

O heart bowed down with sorrow,
  O eyes that long for sight,
There's gladness in believing,
  In Jesus there is light.
"Come unto me all ye that labor
  And are heavy laden, and I will give you rest.
Take my yoke upon you and learn of Me,
  For I am meek and lowly in heart,
  and ye shall find rest unto your souls."

Franklin E. Belden (1895)

...and today, the joy of the Lord is our strength.

We often say in the church family I'm blessed to be a part of, "Sunday is the best day of the week." There's lots of reasons. I hope one is crystal clear to you as this new workweek begins. On Sundays, the joy of the Lord is our song. On Mondays, the joy of the Lord is our strength.

What about you? What did you sing yesterday that is providing strength for today?

TUESDAY

Listen to the Witnesses Today

Therefore, since we are surrounded by so great a cloud of witnesses, let us also lay aside every weight, and sin which clings so closely, and let us run with endurance the race that is set before us… (Heb 12.1)

You'll be surrounded by all sorts of people today. Hopefully, some of them will be fellow "runners," sources of encouragement in the race of faith. Sadly, the majority will be headed in the opposite direction.

But here's something worth remembering today: the "in the flesh" people who surround you aren't the only men and women who can exert influence in your life. You *are* surrounded by a great "cloud of witnesses" who continue to testify in a variety of unique and powerful ways to the surpassing worth of the assurance of things hoped for, the conviction of things not seen. Though they have died, through their faith, they continue to declare that your Creator rewards those who diligently seek him.

Who are these "witnesses," and what are they affirming, even today (Heb 11.4–38)?

Abel. "Acceptable sacrifice to God is always worth it."

Enoch. "You'll never regret living in a way that pleases your heavenly Father."

Noah. "You should take God's warnings seriously."

Abraham. "Even when you don't know the what, where, how, or why, the LORD does."

Sarah. "God is faithful to deliver on his most incredible promises."

Isaac. "The Lord is always able to see farther down the road than we can."

Jacob. "When all hope seems lost, God is often just getting started."

Joseph. "Indulging in sin is never worth compromising what you know to be right."

Amram and **Jochebed**. "Always fear God more than you fear anyone else."

Moses. "It's better to be mistreated with the people of God than to enjoy the fleeting pleasures of sin."

The Israelites of the Exodus. "The Lord can make a way for his people, no matter what."

Joshua and his army. "God's way works, even when it doesn't make sense to us."

Rahab. "God can turn *anyone's* life around."

Gideon. "With God on your side, you're always in the majority."

Barak. "The Lord sometimes delivers in the most unexpected of ways."

Samson. "Let anyone who thinks that he stands take heed lest he fall."

Jephthah. "Faults of the past don't have to destroy the potential of faith in the present."

David. "Allowing the Lord to be the shepherd of your life is the best, most important decision you'll ever make."

Samuel. "Remember that people see the outside, but the Lord sees the heart."

The prophets. "Take care that you do not refuse him who is speaking from heaven."

You'll be surrounded by all sorts of people today, but the men and women you can see with your eyes and hear with your ears aren't the only people worth noticing, remembering, or considering. Open the eyes of faith today. Listen with the blessed assurance of things hoped for. Focus with the time-tested conviction of things not seen.

Though the witnesses in that great cloud have gone on to their reward, through their faith, they continue to speak.

WEDNESDAY

Just Because He Hasn't, Doesn't Mean He Won't

Moses and Aaron went, stood before the most powerful man on the planet, and boldly delivered the straightforward message from the God of Israel, "Let my people go" (Exo 5.1).

Pharaoh's response? "Who is the LORD, that I should obey his voice and let Israel go? I do not know the LORD, and moreover, I will not let Israel go" (5.2). To prove his point, that same day, Pharaoh commanded his taskmasters, "You shall no longer give the people straw to make bricks, as in the past; let them go and gather straw for themselves. But the number of bricks that they made in the past you shall impose on them, you shall by no means reduce it, for they are idle … Let heavier work be laid on the men that they may labor at it and pay no regard to lying words." (5.7–9).

The workload got heavier, the slavery more cruel, and Moses—the supposed savior—got blamed by the very people he'd come to deliver.

> Then Moses turned to the LORD and said, "O Lord, why have you done evil to this people? Why did you ever send me? For since I came to Pharaoh to speak in your name, he has done evil to this people, and you have not delivered your people at all." (5.22–23)

Despair. Doubt. Disillusionment.

When things don't go the way we thought they would, it's easy to despair, to doubt ourselves, and to blame God. I put myself on the line, stepped out in faith, and the outcome I anticipated turns out to be a door slammed in my face? Where were you, God? Why did you do this? Don't you see what's happening? Is this what you wanted? I tried to do the right thing, but you haven't come through at all! Exodus 5 is dripping with despair, doubt, and disillusionment.

But it also stands as a timeless teaching moment and a relevant reminder. Just because God hasn't, doesn't mean he won't. His timing may not line up with our expectations, but that doesn't mean his will isn't right on time. When we can't see, he can. When we don't know, he does. When we're ready to throw in the towel and declare everything a lost cause, he very well may just be getting started.

> But the LORD said to Moses, "Now you shall see … I am the LORD, and I will bring you out from under the burdens of the Egyptians, and I will deliver you from slavery to them, and I will redeem you with an outstretched arm and with great acts of judgment. I will take you to be my people, and I will be your God, and you shall know that I am the LORD your God…" (6.1, 6–7)

Just because he hasn't, doesn't mean he won't. Just because you think he's late, doesn't mean he's not right on time. Just because we're frustrated, doesn't mean he is. Just because I don't understand, doesn't mean he's not on the verge of saying and showing, "Now you shall see."

THURSDAY

Rooted and Grounded … in What?

In what is your heart "rooted and grounded"? That's a question worth thinking about today, especially if you've never thought of your heart in such terms.

The roots of a living thing provide stability and nourishment. Picture the roots of a tall, weathered tree in your mind. Extending much deeper into the ground than the tree is tall, those roots are drawing water and nutrients from the soil, providing life to the trunk, limbs, branches, and leaves. The healthier those roots are, the deeper they grow, and the more stability is provided to the tree above ground. The winds may blow and the branches may bend, but the tree is stable and steadfast because it is firmly "rooted and grounded."

Have you ever thought about your heart having roots? Not the muscle in your chest, but who you really are on the inside—your "inner being." Take a thoughtful listen to Paul's prayer for the first-century disciples in Ephesus.

> …that Christ may dwell in your hearts through faith—that you, being rooted and grounded in love, may have strength to comprehend with all the saints what is the breadth and length and height and depth, and to know the love of Christ that surpasses knowledge, that you may be filled with all the fullness of God. (Eph 3.17–19)

The apostle's earnest desire is that Christians enjoy such a deep, rich, life-giving connection to Jesus that they are "rooted and grounded in love"—the love of Christ "that surpasses knowledge."

So in what is *your* heart rooted and grounded?

Hearts rooted in bitterness yield an ugly harvest of wrath, anger, clamor, and slander.

Hearts rooted in racism don't love the image-bearer of God with a different color of skin as they love themselves.

Hearts rooted in lust desire impurity and sensuality more than they desire God.

Hearts rooted in greed lay up treasures for self on earth at the expense of laying up treasures in heaven.

Hearts rooted in envy are haunted by a spirit of discontentment that takes bountiful blessings for granted.

Hearts rooted in jealousy have a mighty struggle rejoicing with those who are rejoicing.

Hearts rooted in strife won't weep with those who are weeping.

Hearts rooted in enmity struggle to forgive, remaining willfully shortsighted to the abundance of grace they've personally enjoyed.

Darkened hearts rooted in dead soil produce rotten fruit.

But that's not the will of your Father in heaven for you. He is the wise vinedresser who knows how to plant, graft, tend, and prune for our good and his glory. He is willing and able to uproot our hearts from the destructive darkness of sin and replant us in Christ that we might be filled with all the fullness of God, bearing the beautiful fruit of his Spirit. Love. Joy. Peace. Patience. Kindness. Goodness. Faithfulness. Gentleness. Self-control.

Upon what does it all depend? **In what is your heart rooted and grounded?** From what soil are you drawing meaning, purpose, stability, and hope? From what source are you fueling your spirit? Is it refreshing and life-giving or poisonous and soul-parching?

Maybe today is a really good day to dig beneath the surface and honestly check the roots of your heart.

FRIDAY

Surrounded by Doubters and Pessimists, Be a Caleb

The LORD could not have been more clear:

> "Send men to spy out the land of Canaan, which **I am giving** to the people of Israel." (Num 13.2)

Twelve Israelite spies spend forty days scoping out the Promised Land. They transport Exhibit-A of the land's fertility back to their people: a single cluster of grapes so large it must be carried on a pole between two men. Can you imagine how delicious those grapes must have looked to people who had been on a steady diet of wilderness manna?

Then came the spies' report:

> "We came to the land to which you sent us. It flows with milk and honey, and this is its fruit. However, the people who dwell in the land are strong, and the cities are fortified and very large. And besides, we saw the descendants of Anak there. The Amalekites dwell in the land of the Negeb. The Hittites, the Jebusites, and the Amorites dwell in the hill country. And the Canaanites dwell by the sea, and along the Jordan." (13.27–29)

Translation: it's amazing, but there's no way. The obstacles are insurmountable, the challenges too great.

> But Caleb quieted the people before Moses and said, "Let us go up at once and occupy it, for we are well able to overcome it." (13.30)

What made Caleb so confident? He remembered God's promise before the spies were even sent: "**I am giving** the land of Canaan to the people of Israel."

Skeptics and cynics continue to speak up, even among the people of God.

> It won't work. We've already tried. It's someone else's turn. We already know how this is going to turn out. There's no way. We're not able. Not yet. Maybe someday. We're not big enough, strong enough, rich enough, talented enough. Our best days have come and gone. We might as well not even try. It's time to coast. Or give up completely.

As skeptics and cynics continue to speak up, we need Calebs who are willing to respond and remind with faith-filled confidence. If God has said it will work, trust with all your heart that it *will* work. Boldly stand on the promises of the LORD, even if the majority is slipping into despair. If God is on our side, "we are well able."

Surrounded by doubters and pessimists, be a Caleb today.

SATURDAY

He Knows

In Revelation 2 and 3, the resurrected, glorified Jesus Christ communicates individual messages to seven different churches. Each message begins with the same two words: **"I know."** He is the first and the last, the Amen, the Son of God who has eyes like a flame of fire, and he knows. He is the faithful witness, the one who loves us and can free us from our sins by his blood, making us a kingdom, priests to his Father, and he knows. He is the living one who died and is alive forevermore, the holder of the keys of Death and Hades, the ruler of kings on earth who walks among his churches, and he knows.

"I know where you dwell." Jesus described Pergamum as "where Satan's throne is." It's hard to imagine how bad the situation in that city had to be to warrant such a devastating diagnosis. And yet, there were saints—men and women who were holding fast to Jesus' name and refusing to deny his faith. Wherever you are today, whatever the circumstances, however deep the darkness, Jesus knows.

"I know your works." Christians sprinkled throughout Asia were faithfully serving, toiling on, patiently enduring. In the eyes of the world, they had "but little power." And yet, Jesus promises to continue setting before them open doors of opportunity. "Do not fear." "Remember what you have received and keep what you have heard." "Hold fast." "Be faithful." "I am coming." Wherever you are serving today, whatever the obstacles or uncertainties, however small and insufficient you may feel, Jesus knows.

"I know your love." Some had abandoned the love they had at first. Others were lukewarm. Some had the reputation of being alive, but they were dead. Jesus spoke hard-to-hear, straightforward rebukes to many. "Wake up." "You are wretched, pitiable, poor, blind, and naked." "Repent." "Do the works you did at first." But notice the heart behind the rebukes: "Those whom I love, I reprove and discipline." Listen. Jesus knows how badly you've stumbled in the past. He knows how foolish, self-centered, and rebellious you've been. He knows just how far astray from the path of life you've wandered. There are no secrets. He knows. And yet, you were blessed with another day today. The holy and true one who knows you better than you know yourself continues to patiently stand at the door and graciously knock with love in his heart for you. Why?

"I know." Jesus knows how to turn my life around and lead me to victory as more than a conqueror over sin and death. He knows the way to the tree of life. Jesus knows how to clothe you in white garments, give you a new name, and confess you as his own before his Father. Jesus knows how to keep us from being hurt by the second death. "I am he who searches mind and heart." He is alive, never to die again. He cares. He is active, he is coming, and he has promised to give to each of us according to our works.

Which means? It's not enough for *me* to say, **"I know,"** and leave him on the other side of the door. Each message Jesus sends to the churches concludes with the same call: "He who has an ear, let him hear what the Spirit says." The door must be opened. His voice must be heeded. His heart must be trusted. His lead must be followed. And no one can do that for me. But if I will…

> "If anyone hears my voice and opens the door, I will come in to him and eat with him, and he with me. The one who conquers I will grant him to sit with me on my throne, as I also conquered and sat down with my Father on his throne." (Rev 3.20–21)

He knows. May those things we can know about him from Revelation 2 and 3 compel us to stick close to him today.

WEEK THREE

SUNDAY

The Difference Delight Makes

Blessed is the man
   who walks not in the counsel of the wicked,
nor stands in the way of sinners,
   nor sits in the seat of scoffers;
but his **delight** is in the law of the LORD,
   and on his law he meditates day and night.
He is like a tree
   planted by streams of water
that yields its fruit in its season,
   and its leaf does not wither.
In all that he does, he prospers. (Psa 1.1–3)

Delight. What a vivid, emotional word. *Delight* is defined as "a high degree of enjoyment; rapture; something that gives great pleasure."

Don't we naturally meditate on the sources of delight in our lives? If we take a "high degree of enjoyment" from watching football, we anxiously look forward to game time. If I find "great pleasure" in a friend, I'll instinctively yearn just to be in their presence. If what you're feeling on the first tee of a golf course could accurately be described as "rapture," the very next opportunity to tee off will naturally fill your daydreams.

We meditate on the people, possessions, and possibilities our hearts find delightful…

…which means Psalm 1 is worth a serious look today as it continues to encourage readers of all time to slow down for the *right* reasons. Don't walk in the counsel of the wicked or stand in the way of sinners or sit in the seat of scoffers. Instead, slow down, focus, and appreciate the difference delight makes.

Hours devoted to a television screen quickly pass. Human relationships are momentary in the grand scheme of things and even the closest ones can't meet the deepest needs of our souls. The best round of golf on the finest course in the world ultimately boils down to chasing a little white ball into a hole in the ground. Today's shopping thrill is tomorrow's donation to Goodwill.

But the LORD lives on. His wisdom endures. His promises stand. His will sustains. His faithfulness stretches from everlasting to everlasting. His blessings flow like a river through human history. We're reminded of those realities on Sundays as our hearts are stirred with hope and conviction to walk with our God throughout the week.

Then Monday hits with full force. Alarm clocks. Commutes. Deadlines. Stress. Pressure. Meetings. Obligations. Temptations. Distractions. Misplaced priorities. Unplanned hiccups. Overscheduled commitments. Exhaustion. As Monday afternoon turns to Monday evening, I think to myself, "I need something **delightful** to cope with the craziness." And for the rest of the night, I fill my mind with… TV? I seek heart-refreshment in… social media scrolling?

By Tuesday, the life of focused, productive, joy-filled commitment I envisioned on Sunday seems like a distant memory. By Wednesday, my spiritual vitality is withered and my soul's focus is completely blurred.

Why? Because I *need* spiritual nourishment. My heart was created for deep connection to my Creator. And since Sunday? What have I delighted in? Wicked things? Filthy things? Foolish things? Maybe even lots and lots of "good" things, but so *many* "good" things that the "best" things have been crowded out and left behind.

I've been walking for days through a harsh desert without a drop of living water.

Maybe today is a good day to be reminded that I'm not invincible, physically or spiritually. Without the blessings that flow from a healthy relationship with God, I can camp on the edge of the cliff only so long before erosion begins to have a disastrous effect.

Maybe that's exactly how your heart feels today. Shriveled. Heavy. Struggling to hope. Far from peace. Bitter. Full of weeds. Weary. Parched. Why? Could I ask a personal question? In what have you delighted since last Sunday? You've meditated on the people, possessions, and possibilities your heart finds delightful. **Could it be that you have a critical delight deficiency?**

Maybe Psalm 1 is the spiritual oasis you've needed for a long, long time. Blessed is the man who delights in the LORD. Blessed is the woman who meditates on his good will for her life. That man is like a tree. It's as if that woman has been planted, deeply rooted by streams of water. He yields fruit. Her leaves don't wither. The deepest needs of his heart are abundantly supplied by an infinite Source of love and joy. There are plenty of things in the world she can't control, but her soul is settled and satisfied.

That's the difference delight makes.

MONDAY

Like Water in a Dry Place

Behold, a king will reign in righteousness,
    and princes will rule in justice.
Each will be like a hiding place from the wind,
    a shelter from the storm,
like streams of water in a dry place,
    like the shade of a great rock in a weary land. (Isa 32.1–2)

Glimpses of the coming Messiah can be caught throughout Isaiah's prophecy. Immanuel, born of a virgin. A great light dawning on people who have dwelt in deep darkness. The government resting upon the shoulders of the One who will be called Wonderful Counselor, Mighty God, Everlasting Father, Prince of Peace. A shoot from the stump of Jesse that will bear the fruit of righteousness as the Spirit of the Lord rests upon him. And in Isaiah 32, another precious glimpse. "Behold, a king will reign in righteousness."

Notice what those who submit themselves to this true and rightful King will find and perhaps grow to be like: a hiding place from the wind. A shelter from the storm. Streams of water in a dry place. The shade of a great rock in a weary land.

Isn't this the impact disciples of Jesus are supposed to have on the world today? Aren't these the environments we ought to create with his help and maintain in his name?

- Homes founded on righteousness that are like hiding places from the wind

- Respect for all image-bearers that serves as a kind of relational-shelter from the storm
- In-person interactions and social media feeds that are like streams of water in a dry place
- Churches that are like the shade of a great rock in a weary land

Read Isaiah 32. As long as this world stands, fools will continue to speak folly and some hearts will be busy with iniquity (32.6). Scoundrels will continue to plan wicked schemes and the poor will be ruined with lying words (32.7).

> But he who is noble plans noble things,
>   and on noble things he stands. (32.8)

Noble living shaped by the noble principles of a noble King. It will be like water in a dry place, and it will have a noble impact on the parched world around us. Sounds a lot like Philippians 4.8–9, doesn't it?

> Finally, brothers, whatever is true, whatever is honorable, whatever is just, whatever is pure, whatever is lovely, whatever is commendable, if there is any excellence, if there is anything worthy of praise, think about these things. What you have learned and received and heard and seen in me—practice these things, and the God of peace will be with you.

Think about these things, practice these things, and the King just might use you as a spiritual oasis for someone else today. In the grand scheme of things, what could be more important?

TUESDAY

You Have to Push Through the Crowd

And a great crowd followed [Jesus] and thronged about him.
(Mark 5.24)

You know what big crowds are like, don't you? What word or phrase comes to mind when you think of a "great crowd" of people? Unruly? Exciting? Noisy? Impatient? Unpredictable? Pushy? Hard to navigate? Whatever the word, get that buzz and vibe in your mind. That's our scene in Mark 5.

And there was a woman who had had a discharge of blood for twelve years, and who had suffered much under many physicians, and had spent all that she had, and was no better but rather grew worse. (5.25–26)

Imagine being that woman. Imagine the loud, excited, chaotic throng of people in every direction. Imagine the desperation. Imagine everything you'd have to do just to avoid *losing* ground, being pushed and pulled further away from Jesus. Imagine how hard it must have been to get anywhere *near* Jesus on days like that day. And yet, somehow…

She had heard the reports about Jesus and came up behind him in the crowd and touched his garment. For she said, "If I touch even his garments, I will be made well." And immediately the flow of blood dried up, and she felt in her body that she was healed of her disease. (5.27–29)

Can you imagine?

And Jesus, perceiving in himself that power had gone out from him, immediately turned about in the crowd and said, "Who touched my garments?" And his disciples said to him, "You see the crowd pressing around you, and yet you say, 'Who touched me?'" And he looked around to see who had done it. But the woman, knowing what had happened to her, came in fear and trembling and fell down before him and told him the whole truth. And he said to her, "Daughter, your faith has made you well; go in peace, and be healed of your disease." (5.30–34)

Let's make this personal. Every day of your life, a great "crowd" can easily form between you and the Son of God—a throng that is constantly pulling, pushing, distracting, and interrupting you.

Appointments. Bills. Kids. Breakfast. Traffic. Expectations. Deadlines. Expense reports. Quarterly reviews. Final exams. Friends. Frustrations. Politics. Facebook. Twitter. Instagram. Pinterest. TikTok. CNN. Fox News. MSNBC. ESPN. The Today Show. Lunch. Email. Text messages. Podcasts. Sports. Recitals. Hospital visits. Homework. Housework. Mowing. Shoveling. Landscaping. Weeds. Decorations. Repairs. Interruptions. Supper. Dishes. Planning. Taxes. Phone calls. Family time. Bath time. Snack time. Bed time.

If you're not intentional and deliberate, this "crowd" will easily and aggressively fill the space between you and Jesus… today… this week… this month… this season… this year… for the next few years… If you simply go with the flow, this "crowd" will *keep you from* Jesus as long as you live.

You know what that means? **You have to push through the crowd.** You have to recognize your need. You have to feel the desperation. You have to be hungry and thirsty. You have to set your eyes on your Savior. **You have to push.**

I'm guessing it's a busy day, in the middle of a busy week, in the midst of a busy season of life.

Don't lose sight of him.

You *need* to hear him. You *need* to talk with him. You *need* to walk with him. You *need* to be refreshed by him. You can't snap your fingers and make the "crowd" disappear, but you *can* push through the crowd. Prioritize, purge, sacrifice, deny yourself, do whatever you must do to maintain consistent, authentic contact with him. **Why?** It may be inconvenient. Sometimes, it's going to be really, really tough. **Is it worth it?**

It is if you believe he still recognizes the determined touch of faith.

"Daughter, your faith has made you well; go in peace, and be healed."

Push through the crowd today.

WEDNESDAY

I Want Eyes Like My Father's Eyes Today

When Habakkuk the prophet addressed the Lord, the Holy One, he described him in these terms:

> "You who are of purer eyes than to see evil
>   and cannot look at wrong…" (Hab 1.13)

I want eyes like my Father's eyes today. How about you?

Granted, I can't control everything that comes into my field of vision today. But I *can* control whether or not I will gaze. I have a choice between following or ignoring the clickbait. My eyes are the gates of my mind and when I willfully open those gates and yield access, access is granted because I *chose* to grant it.

My Creator is of purer eyes than to see evil and cannot look at wrong. He is the Holy One. He calls *me* to be holy in all my conduct (1 Pet 1.15–16). In order to answer that call I must "prepare" my mind "for action," determining to be "sober-minded" and "setting" my hope "fully on the grace" that will be brought to me "at the revelation of Jesus Christ" (1 Pet 1.13).

All of which means: if I want eyes like my Father's eyes today, the time to prepare is **now**. The decision to be sober-minded is new every morning. The gates of my mind must be secured–"I have made a covenant with my eyes" (Job 31.1)–and the rightful King must be "set" on the throne of my heart. "My hope is built on nothing less than Jesus' blood and righteousness."

I want eyes like my Father's eyes today. How about you?

THURSDAY

Living Rest Stops for the Heaven-Bound

In Acts 21, Paul's third missionary journey is coming to a close. He's headed for Jerusalem and almost certain danger. Multiple people have urged him not to go. His answer?

> "What are you doing, weeping and breaking my heart? For I am ready not only to be imprisoned but even to die in Jerusalem for the name of the Lord Jesus." (Acts 21.13)

It's incredible faith and determination. But notice the "fuel" of encouragement Paul got along the way.

In Tyre.

Having sought out the disciples, we stayed there for seven days… they all, with wives and children, accompanied us until we were outside the city. And kneeling down on the beach, we prayed… (Acts 21.4–5)

In Ptolemais.

…we greeted the brothers and stayed with them for one day. (Acts 21.7)

In Caesarea.

…we entered the house of Philip the evangelist, who was one of the seven, and stayed with him… for many days… (Acts 21.8, 10)

In Jerusalem.

Some of the disciples from Caesarea went with us, bringing us to the house of Mnason of Cyprus, an early disciple, with whom we should lodge. When we had come to Jerusalem, the brothers received us gladly. (Acts 21.16–17)

We don't even know the names of most of these people. They were just ordinary men, women, and children. But they were also disciples of Jesus and they served as spiritual rest stops for Paul. They welcomed. They shared their possessions and property. They refreshed. They prayed. They listened. They rejoiced and wept. And as ordinary people served as the hands and feet of Jesus, they provided the fuel of encouragement to an apostle's heart.

God knows what their names were. He knows yours too. He will use all-too-ordinary people all over the world this week to provide spiritual fuel for the heaven-bound.

What can you do to be a son or daughter of encouragement today?

FRIDAY

"I Appreciate You"

She's my favorite worker at the Post Office. I'm typically in our local branch at least twice a week. She's one of several who serve behind the counter, but she's the only one who consistently makes me smile. Postal workers aren't notorious for making customers smile, but she does. Every time she processes a package or answers a P.O. Box question or sells a book of stamps, she says the same thing as her customers begin to walk away into the rest of their day: "I appreciate you." Just three words, but she stands out because of them.

> A word fitly spoken is like apples of gold in a setting of silver. (Prov 25.11)

Our words *can* make a difference, serving as a refreshment to those who hear them. We are surrounded by people who don't hear refreshing words very often.

- "I appreciate you."
- "I notice you."
- "I care about you."
- "I'm here for you."
- "I love you."
- "I thank you."

If anyone ought to serve as a fountain of refreshing words in an arid world, it's Christians!

Who might you refresh with words fitly spoken today?

SATURDAY

The Faces of Romans 16

Bible passages like Romans 16.1–15 can be difficult to read, especially out loud. Just take a look at the names referenced by the apostle Paul:

> Phoebe. Prisca. Aquila. Epaenetus. Andronicus. Junia. Ampliatus. Urbanus. Stachys. Apelles. Aristobulus. Herodion. Narcissus. Tryphaena. Tryphosa. Persis. Rufus. Asyncritus. Phlegon. Hermes. Patrobas. Hermas. Philologus. Julia. Nereus. Olympas.

Get asked to read this section of Scripture in a Bible class and the challenge is likely to give most of us a hot flash.

Maybe in our personal Bible reading, as we come to sections of Scripture like this, we see the long list of hard-to-pronounce names and gloss right over the conclusion of *Romans*, skipping straight to the introduction of *1 Corinthians*. After all, why spend time wading through the names of people who lived such a long time ago and with whom we seem to have so little in common?

But what if we slowed down long enough to really look at, notice, and think about the descriptions immediately before and after those hard-to-pronounce names? Listen to the way Paul described these men and women...

> Our sister ... a servant of the church ... a patron of many ... fellow workers in Christ Jesus ... beloved ... who has worked hard for you ... in Christ before me ... approved in Christ ... workers in the Lord ... who has worked hard in the Lord ... chosen in the Lord ... who has been a mother to me as well ...

Descriptions like that ought to remind us that these were real people—brothers and sisters in Christ—with faces, stories, struggles, homes, hopes, and fears. Their faith had not only transformed *their* lives, it was having a ripple effect for good throughout the world. Why do we even know the names of Tryphaena and Tryphosa today? Because they were "workers in the Lord." We *don't* know the name of Rufus' mother, but we *do* know, two thousand years after the fact, that she had been a mother to Paul as well.

I recently sat with a great group of 20-somethings in my office. We opened our Bibles to Romans 16 and just went in a circle, reading verse by verse through this difficult list of names. Then we took a "field trip" down the hall to the big picture board in the foyer of the church building, full of the faces that make up our church family. I went around the circle again and asked them to put modern faces to those ancient descriptions...

Our sister ... a servant of the church ... a patron of many ... fellow workers in Christ Jesus ... beloved ... who has worked hard for you ... in Christ before me ... approved in Christ ... workers in the Lord ... who has worked hard in the Lord ... chosen in the Lord ... who has been a mother to me as well ...

And suddenly, it was a little easier to look at that ancient text with fresh light. The faces have changed. The names are obviously different. Empires have risen and fallen as centuries have passed. But God's kingdom is alive and well as the fruit of the Spirit continues to be borne in the lives of men and women whose allegiance has been wholeheartedly pledged to King Jesus.

As you come to passages like Romans 16, don't be so intimated by the names that you fail to notice how the people behind the names are described. These were servants of the Lord, kingdom citizens, and blessings to the people around them.

In fact, maybe today is a good day to make that personal. Take a little while to thumb or scroll through your congregation's picture directory. Notice the servants. As you look at the faces, marvel at the fact that you've been blessed with so many brothers and sisters! Thank God for the good examples of those who were in Christ before you. Remember those who've gone on to their reward after working hard for the Lord. Then use that little exercise as fuel to verbalize your appreciation for someone who has made a real difference in your life.

From the faces of Romans 16 to the faces of our brethren in the twenty-first century, what a blessing to be a part of the ransomed people for God from every tribe and language and people and nation!

WEEK FOUR

SUNDAY

The God Who is Willing to Bear the Burdens You Are Willing to Cast

Burdens. Psalm 55 is full of heavy burdens.

I am restless in my complaint and I moan. (55.2)

[The wicked] drop trouble upon me,
and in anger they bear a grudge against me. (55.3)

My heart is in anguish within me;
the terrors of death have fallen upon me. (55.4)

Fear and trembling come upon me,
and horror overwhelms me. (55.5)

I see violence and strife in the city. (55.9)

Oppression and fraud
do not depart from its marketplace. (55.11)

For it is not an enemy who taunts me—
then I could bear it;
it is not an adversary who deals insolently with me—
then I could hide from him.
But it is you, a man, my equal,
my companion, my familiar friend.
We used to take sweet counsel together;
within God's house we walked in the throng. (55.12–14)

Heavy burdens. Restlessness. A gathering enemy. Oppression. Grudges. Anguish. Fear. Violence. Strife. Fraud. Taunts. Betrayal. Psalm 55 is *full* of heavy burdens.

And yet, David wholeheartedly believes that he, a mere mortal, can address the Lord of the universe, "he who is enthroned from of old" (55.19), with confidence.

> Give ear to my prayer, O God,
>   and hide not yourself from my plea for mercy!
> Attend to me, and answer me. (55.1–2)

> I call to God,
>   and the LORD will save me.
> Evening and morning and at noon
>   I utter my complaint and moan,
>   and he hears my voice. (55.16–17)

Incredible. Perhaps even *more* incredible? David encourages us to do the same.

> Cast your burden on the LORD,
>   and he will sustain you;
> he will never permit
>   the righteous to be moved. (55.22)

This is the God who is willing to bear the burdens you are willing to cast. Doesn't God's own Son make that clear?

> "Come to me, all who labor and are heavy laden, and I will give you rest. Take my yoke upon you, and learn from me, for I am gentle and lowly in heart, and you will find rest for your souls. For my yoke is easy, and my burden is light." (Matt 11.28–30)

He is willing to bear the burdens you are willing to cast. The burden of past sin.

> There is therefore now no condemnation for those who are in Christ Jesus. (Rom 8.1)

The burden of present trials.

If God is for us, who can be against us? (Rom 8.31)

Who is to condemn? Christ Jesus is the one who died—more than that, who was raised—who is at the right hand of God, who indeed is interceding for us. Who shall separate us from the love of Christ? Shall tribulation, or distress, or persecution, or famine, or nakedness, or danger, or sword? (Rom 8.34–35)

No, in all these things we are more than conquerors through him who loved us. (Rom 8.37)

The burden of anxieties over the future.

The sufferings of this present time are not worth comparing with the glory that is to be revealed to us. (Rom 8.18)

For I am sure that neither death nor life, nor angels nor rulers, nor things present nor things to come, nor powers, nor height nor depth, nor anything else in all creation, will be able to separate us from the love of God in Christ Jesus our Lord. (Rom 8.38–39)

This is the assurance that frees us to cast.

Heavy burdens are a part of post-Genesis 3 life. When I go a day, a week, a month without prayer, I'm acting as if I can carry those burdens on my own. Truth is, I can't. Grace is, I don't have to. "Cast your burden on the Lord." If I'm willing to cast it in faith, he's willing and able to bear it. Just listen…

Humble yourselves, therefore, under the mighty hand of God so that at the proper time he may exalt you, casting all your anxieties on him, because he cares for you. (1 Pet 5.6–7)

MONDAY

If You Never Open the Box…

And Hilkiah the high priest said to Shaphan the secretary, "I have found the Book of the Law in the house of the Lord." And Hilkiah gave the book to Shaphan, and he read it. And Shaphan the secretary came to [Josiah], and reported to the king, "Your servants have emptied out the money that was found in the house and have delivered it into the hand of the workmen who have the oversight of the house of the Lord." Then Shaphan the secretary told the king, "Hilkiah the priest has given me a book." And Shaphan read it before the king.

When the king heard the words of the Book of the Law, he tore his clothes. (2 Kings 22.8–11)

Maybe you saw the headlines: **"Something Borrowed, Something Mixed-Up."** In January 2021, Wendie Taylor was watching TV with her 12-year-old daughter when the subject of weddings came up. Wendie's daughter mentioned that she had never actually seen her mother's wedding dress. Sure, she'd seen pictures, but never the dress itself.

So, Wendie decided to go get the special box out of storage. As she was working to get it down, she realized that even *she* had never actually looked in it since picking the package up from a professional garment preservation service. For 14 years, the dress had been in a sealed, unopened box.

And when Wendie finally opened the box? She discovered that the dress she'd been holding onto wasn't hers. "It's a beautiful dress," she told news agencies who picked up the story after it went viral on social media, "it's just not my dress." Had she never opened the box, Wendie would have assumed she knew what was in it for the rest of her life. And she would have been wrong.

While it's easy to shake your head at Wendie's assumption, isn't it even easier to live day by day with bigger assumptions? In fact, it doesn't require anything at all from us to live with much greater, more eternally-significant assumptions. "I know what I'm doing. I'm good where I'm at. I know what tomorrow holds. If there is a God, I'm sure he's happy with the life I'm living."

How many will walk through today with those assumptions, never taking the time to open God's Book and examine what he's actually said? The life I'm building may be more than sufficient—even beautiful in my own eyes—but that doesn't mean it's life the way my Creator meant it to be, and my own assumptions don't make it so.

Listen. You were created for a relationship with your Creator. Don't try to build it on something borrowed or inherited. Just because you've been handed a box labeled **"The Good Life"** or **"Salvation"** or **"Acceptable Worship,"** don't assume you know what's on the inside of that package. Assume, and you very well may end up with something mixed-up.

Open God's Book for yourself. Explore. Confirm. Develop a real spiritual appetite of your own. Stay curious, hungry, and thirsty. You can be God's and God can be yours, but if you never open the "box," who knows what you're missing?

I believe you're missing right things. Wise things. Corrective things. Needed things. Wondrous things.

TUESDAY

Be More Than a Messenger; Be a Model

Preachers did important work on Sunday. As those charged with teaching "what accords with sound doctrine" (Tit 2.1):

- We challenged older men to be sober-minded, dignified, self-controlled, sound in faith, in love, and in steadfastness (2.2)
- We taught older women to be reverent in behavior, not slanderers or slaves to much wine, but teachers of what is good (2.3)
- We encouraged young women to love their husbands and children, to be self-controlled, pure, working at home, kind, and submissive to their own husbands, that the word of God may not be reviled (2.4–5)
- We urged younger men to be self-controlled (2.6)

That's eternally-important work and my guess is the minds of most messengers are already on the next opportunity to teach more of what accords with sound doctrine.

But could I encourage my fellow messengers not to overlook or neglect Titus 2.7–8? We taught foundational truths with roots in Titus 2.1–6 and expected others to listen on Sunday. On Monday and Tuesday, are we listening to the Spirit of God as he reminds us to be *more* than messengers?

> Show yourself in all respects to be a model of good works, and in your teaching show integrity, dignity, and sound speech that

cannot be condemned, so that an opponent may be put to shame, having nothing evil to say about us.

Be about more than standing on a stage on Sundays. "Show yourself in all respects to be a model of good works" throughout this week. In person, in your home, in your office, at the grocery store, in the stands, on social media, show integrity, dignity, and sound speech that cannot be condemned. Be more than a messenger; be a model worthy of imitation because you're imitating Christ (1 Cor 11.1).

If the Lord wills, we'll speak out against the evil of the world next Sunday. By all means, prepare to "declare these things; exhort and rebuke with all authority. Let no one disregard you" (2.15). But in the meantime, let's also guard against the evil that can ravage our own examples. "In everything," may *we* "adorn the doctrine of God our Savior" that we so love to share with others.

WEDNESDAY

Paradise Was a Package Deal

When "the whole land" lies before you, what do you choose?

Genesis 13 describes a time when the flocks, herds, tents, and possessions of Abram and his nephew Lot "were so great that they could not dwell together." The same land was simply unable to support both of them and strife was beginning to break out between their herdsmen.

> Then Abram said to Lot, "Let there be no strife between you and me, and between your herdsmen and my herdsmen, for we are kinsmen. Is not the whole land before you? Separate yourself from me. If you take the left hand, then I will go to the right, or if you take the right hand, then I will go to the left." (13.8–9)

The elder could have flexed his patriarchal muscles and told the younger how it was going to be, but he gave the gift of the choice to his nephew.

So, when "the whole land" lies before you, what do you choose?

> Lot lifted up his eyes and saw that the Jordan Valley was well watered everywhere like the garden of the LORD, like the land of Egypt, in the direction of Zoar. (This was before the LORD destroyed Sodom and Gomorrah.) So Lot chose for himself all the Jordan Valley, and Lot journeyed east. Thus they separated from each other. Abram settled in the land of Canaan, while Lot settled among the cities of the valley and moved his tent as far

as Sodom. Now the men of Sodom were wicked, great sinners against the Lord. (13.10–13)

What an opportunity for Lot! How lush must this valley have been to merit a "like the garden of the Lord" description? Well-watered. Green. Fertile. Paradise. **But at what cost?** If you're familiar with the rest of Lot's story, you know just how great that cost turned out to be.

Maybe today is a good moment to remember: life is connected. Choices have consequences. Weighty ambitions create far-reaching ripple effects.

"If I follow the lead of these friends, is their influence going to push me towards wisdom or pull me towards foolishness?"

"If I choose that college, will I have the godly support system I need?"

"If I date that person, does it matter whether or not they love God?"

"If I marry that person, are they going to help me get to heaven?"

"If we move to ... what sort of influences will meet our children head-on?"

"If I take that job, what temptations will fly in tandem with the opportunities?"

"If I accept this added responsibility, will I still be able to maintain and nurture what matters most?"

"If we retire here, will we remain as active and effective for the kingdom as we can be?"

Without a doubt, wherever disciples of Jesus live, go to school, work, and interact, there will be challenges. We live "in" a world we are not "of"–a world drowning in the desires of the flesh, the desires of the eyes, and the pride of life. Our citizenship is in heaven, and from it we await our Savior, but our choices in the meantime have very real consequences.

Lot "lifted up his eyes and saw" what looked like paradise, but paradise was a package-deal. As he settled among the cities of the valley and moved his tent as far as Sodom, the influential pull was strong "against the LORD."

> Look carefully then how you walk, not as unwise but as wise, making the best use of the time, because the days are evil. Therefore do not be foolish, but understand what the will of the Lord is. (Eph 5.15–17)

Today is a good day to pray for wisdom, endurance, and the boldness necessary to unashamedly shine as lights in a dark world where the pull "against the LORD" continues to be very strong.

THURSDAY

Step By Step With the One Who Knows How

"He knows how…"

If my car has broken down, I want someone who knows what they're doing under the hood.

If I'm flying across the country at 30,000 feet, I want someone who knows what they're doing in the cockpit.

If my daughter is going into surgery, I want someone who knows what they're doing in the operating room.

"He knows how." "She knows what she's doing." We find comfort, reassurance, and hope in those words.

With that simple principle in mind, could I encourage you to tuck 2 Peter 2.9 into the pocket of your heart and return to it off and on throughout the day?

…then the Lord knows how to rescue the godly from trials.

He knows how. The godly have trials in front of them this week. *You* will encounter trials on the trail ahead. For 2,000 years, these God-breathed words of comfort, reassurance, and hope have been preserved for any and all who are willing to be shaped and governed by them. The Lord knows exactly where you are. He knows where he's going. He knows how to rescue, sustain, and lead his people all the way to glory.

Why, then, would we push ahead, lag behind, or take one careless step without him this week?

FRIDAY

The Lesson of the Lambs in Leviticus

Leviticus—the third book of the Bible—is a bloody, bloody book. God is delivering law after law about the sacrifices his chosen people were to offer—burnt offerings, grain offerings, peace offerings, sin offerings, and guilt offerings. It's a challenging book for us to read. But every once in a while, we get clear glimpses of what this whole sacrificial system was really about.

Take a moment to read Leviticus 17.11 and 17.14–16.

"For the life of the flesh is in the blood, and I have given it for you on the altar to make atonement for your souls, for **it is the blood that makes atonement** by the life."

"For the life of every creature is its blood: its blood is its life. Therefore I have said to the people of Israel, You shall not eat the blood of any creature, for the life of every creature is its blood. Whoever eats it shall be cut off. And every person who eats what dies of itself or what is torn by beasts, whether he is a native or a sojourner, shall wash his clothes and bathe himself in water and be unclean until the evening; then he shall be clean. But if he does not wash them or bathe his flesh, **he shall bear his iniquity.**"

Blood. Why all the bloody sacrifices?

"The life of the flesh is in the blood," and God was "giving it for you"–granting this sacrificial system–"to make atonement for your souls." If the descendants of Abraham would follow his lead by faith, shed blood could make atonement. Unblemished life could be sacrificed to cover sins.

And if a person *didn't* follow the LORD's gracious lead? "He shall bear his iniquity." No sacrifice, no atonement, only personal responsibility for one's own transgressions.

Leviticus is a tough book to read and it's easy to get lost in the details. But when we begin to wrap our minds around what God is really saying, great New Testament truths become all the more clear and powerful. For instance,

> But when Christ appeared as a high priest of the good things that have come, then through the greater and more perfect tent (not made with hands, that is, not of this creation) he entered once for all into the holy places, not by means of the blood of goats and calves but by means of his own blood, thus securing an eternal redemption. For if the blood of goats and bulls, and the sprinkling of defiled persons with the ashes of a heifer, sanctify for the purification of the flesh, how much more will the blood of Christ, who through the eternal Spirit offered himself without blemish to God, purify our conscience from dead works to serve the living God. (Heb 9.11–14)

Life is in the blood, and the perfect life has been sacrificed, once for all, to make atonement for our sins.

If I turn my back on the sacrifice of God's own Son, there is no other sacrifice, no means of atonement, only personal accountability to bear the soul-crushing weight of my own transgressions.

Praise God that someone—not some*thing*, Someone—was willing to bear our griefs and carry our sorrows.

SATURDAY

The Saddest Summary of a Life You Can Imagine

In Revelation 9, we read one of the saddest summaries imaginable. In a vision revealed by God himself, John is being made to see some dark and terrible things. A bottomless pit from which billows the smoke of a great furnace. The sun and the air, darkened. Terrible locusts that torment and devour unlike anything experienced in the natural world. A king named Destruction. A third of mankind, destroyed. Can you imagine what John is feeling in the pit of his stomach as this terrifying vision unfolds?

But notice the last two verses of Revelation 9.

> The rest of mankind, who were not killed by these plagues, **did not repent** of the works of their hands nor give up worshiping demons and idols of gold and silver and bronze and stone and wood, which cannot see or hear or walk, **nor did they repent** of their murders or their sorceries or their sexual immorality or their thefts. (9.20–21)

What's the saddest thing you can imagine being on someone's tombstone? I'm not sure I can think of a sadder summary than, **"He refused to turn."**

My teenager is learning to drive. Fundamental to the skill of driving is knowing when to stop and turn. Maybe you'll go hiking this Summer. Everyone realizes how foolish it would be to start walking along a mountain path and refuse to turn as the trail bears left *away* from the edge of a sheer cliff. Parents, college counselors, financial advisors, preachers of the gospel, shepherds of local churches—they all encourage us to turn when it is in our best interest, especially as we're approaching danger and destruction.

But the choice to turn is a personal choice. Beyond the warning signs, the blinking lights, the reasoned pleas, and the efforts of others to "wake us up," repentance is always a personal decision.

Think about it. Once the opportunities of life have been spent, what sadder summary could there be than, **"She refused to turn"**?

His ways are not our ways; his thoughts are infinitely higher than our thoughts, but we *know* this: our Creator is so very patient, not wishing that anyone should perish, but that all should reach repentance (2 Pet 3.9).

Do you need to make a course adjustment today?

WEEK FIVE

SUNDAY

Don't Settle for Pleasures With an Expiration Date

You make known to me the path of life;
  in your presence there is fullness of joy;
  at your right hand are pleasures forevermore. (Psa 16.11)

Multiple paths lie before us each and every day; but not every path leads to life.

Promises of joy are relentlessly advertised at every turn; but not all joys are full.

Pleasures of varieties beyond our wildest imaginations are alluringly offered with easy access, no strings attached, and minimal consequences; but not all pleasures last forevermore.

The path of life? Your Creator has revealed it in his word. Fullness of joy? It can be found in his presence. Pleasures forevermore? They are graciously available at his right hand.

Which means?

I can't ignore him, pave my own trail, and end up with life. I can't forsake him, embrace idols, and experience joy to the fullest. I can't rebel against him, indulge myself as if I'm King of the universe, and inherit pleasures forevermore.

Not every path leads to life. Not all joys are full. Not every pleasure lasts forever. But on *His* path? Life. In *His* presence? Fullness of joy. At *His* right hand? Pleasures. Forevermore.

Listen to Psalm 16.11 today. Don't concede life. Don't chase cheap joy. Don't settle for pleasures with an expiration date. Follow his lead, abide in him, entrust your soul to him, and you'll miss out on some things. But they can't even begin to compare with what you'll gain.

MONDAY

With What Sort of Heart Will You Respond When the Spears Are Hurled in Your Direction?

Saul was king in Israel but consumed with jealousy. Women in his kingdom had been heard celebrating,

> "Saul has struck down his thousands,
>   and David his ten thousands." (1 Sam 18.7)

And Saul was very angry, and this saying displeased him. He said, "They have ascribed to David ten thousands, and to me they have ascribed thousands, and what more can he have but the kingdom?" And Saul eyed David from that day on.

The next day a harmful spirit from God rushed upon Saul, and he raved within his house while David was playing the lyre, as he did day by day. Saul had his spear in his hand. And Saul hurled the spear, for he thought, "I will pin David to the wall." But David evaded him twice. (1 Sam 18.7–11)

In those moments, David had a choice.

- He had already been anointed by Samuel (16.1–13)
- The Spirit of the Lord had rushed upon David (16.13)
- The Spirit of the Lord had departed from Saul (16.14)
- David had shown himself courageous by standing up to and slaying Goliath when no one else would, including Saul (1 Sam 17)

- Though he had been anointed by Samuel, David continued to humbly play the lyre for the refreshment and well-being of mad King Saul

To this point, David had been a model of doing the right thing, at the right time, for the right reasons. And what did he receive from Saul in return for his integrity and loyalty? A spear, hurled in his direction—not once, but twice.

In those moments, David had a choice.

1. Retaliate and become king in the image of Saul.
2. Wait on the Lord, leave vengeance in divine hands, continue doing what is right, and become king in the image of God.

The point? "Spears" will occasionally be hurled in *your* direction. Perhaps they are even hurled frequently. In those moments, you also have a choice.

1. Retaliate as a man or woman whose mind is set on the things of this world.
2. Respond as a son or daughter of God whose mind is set on the glories of heaven.

Romans 12.14–21 describes, in very practical terms, the way men and women whose hearts beat in harmony with God will respond.

Bless those who persecute you; bless and do not curse them. Rejoice with those who rejoice, weep with those who weep. Live in harmony with one another. Do not be haughty, but associate with the lowly. Never be wise in your own sight. Repay no one evil for evil, but give thought to do what is honorable in the sight of all. If possible, so far as it depends on you, live peaceably with all. Beloved, never avenge yourselves, but leave it to the wrath of God, for it is written, "Vengeance is mine, I will repay, says the Lord." To the contrary, "if your enemy is hungry, feed him; if he is thirsty, give him something to drink; for by so doing you will heap burning coals on his head." Do not be overcome by evil, but overcome evil with good.

When "spears" are hurled in your direction, you always have a choice. "With what sort of heart will I respond?" Choose carefully. Choose wisely. Who knows what evil might be overcome if you choose the good?

TUESDAY

The Third Day

On the third day... (John 2.1)

Have you ever noticed that detail in John's Gospel? It's curious to me because of what comes before.

In John 1.19–28, John the Baptist reveals to priests and Levites sent by the Pharisees in Jerusalem, "I baptize with water, but among you stands one you do not know, even he who comes after me, the strap of whose sandal I am not worthy to untie."

"The next day" John sees Jesus coming toward him and proclaims, "Behold, the Lamb of God, who takes away the sin of the world!" (1.29–34)

"The next day" two of John's disciples begin following Jesus (1.35–42).

"The next day" Jesus decides to go to Galilee (1.43–51).

And how does John 2 begin? **"On the third day..."**

Is John simply documenting for us what happened day-by-day from the start of Jesus' ministry? Does he make an irrelevant, coincidental shift in language from "the next day," "the next day," "the next day," to "the third day"? Or is there something more, especially in light of the way his Gospel began?

"In the beginning" (John 1.1). That's how Genesis 1.1 begins.

"God *said*," Genesis 1.3 continues. John 1.1–3 reads, "In the beginning was the Word, and the Word was with God, and the Word was God. He was in the beginning with God. All things were made through him, and without him was not any thing made that was made."

What did God say in Genesis 1.3? "Let there be light," and there was light. "And God saw that the light was good. And God separated the light from the darkness" (1.4). How does John go on to describe "the Word"? "In him was life, and the life was the light of men. The light shines in the darkness, and the darkness has not overcome it" (John 1.4–5).

On the second day of Genesis 1, God made the expanse and separated the waters from the waters. And on the third day?

> God said, "Let the waters under the heavens be gathered together into one place, and let the dry land appear." And it was so. God called the dry land Earth, and the waters that were gathered together he called Seas. And God saw that it was good.
>
> And God said, "Let the earth sprout vegetation, plants yielding seed, and fruit trees bearing fruit in which is their seed, each according to its kind, on the earth." And it was so. The earth brought forth vegetation, plants yielding seed according to their own kinds, and trees bearing fruit in which is their seed, each according to its kind. And God saw that it was good. And there was evening and there was morning, the third day. (1.9–13)

Where was Jesus "on the third day" in John's Gospel?

> On the third day there was a wedding at Cana in Galilee, and the mother of Jesus was there. Jesus also was invited to the wedding with his disciples. When the wine ran out, the mother of Jesus said to him, "They have no wine." And Jesus said to her, "Woman what does this have to do with me? My hour has not yet come." His mother said to the servants, "Do whatever he tells you." (2.1–5)

Well what did she expect him to do? What could *anybody* do? There *was* wine, now there **wasn't**. And what did this have to do with Jesus, just a guest at the wedding?

Now there were six stone water jars there for the Jewish rites of purification, each holding twenty or thirty gallons. Jesus said to the servants, "Fill the jars with water." And they filled them up to the brim. And he said to them, "Now draw some out and take it to the master of the feast." So they took it. When the master of the feast tasted the water now become wine, and did not know where it came from (though the servants who had drawn the water knew), the master of the feast called the bridegroom and said to him, "Everyone serves the good wine first, and when people have drunk freely, then the poor wine. But you have kept the good wine until now." (2.6–10)

And what does John want us to see, believe, and understand?

This, the first of his signs, Jesus did at Cana in Galilee, and manifested his glory. (2.11)

Glory manifested. Power revealed. Transcendence made evident. "Who then is this?" his disciples will repeatedly ask. Who is able to turn water into wine?

John has already introduced us in the prologue of his Gospel. The One who was "in the beginning." The Word through whom all things were made. The true light. The gatherer of the waters and sculptor of dry land. Turning water into wine is no challenge for the One who made the vegetation, plants, and fruit trees sprout from nothing in the first place. He is the God of the third day, and every day, forevermore.

So the Jews said to him, "What sign do you show us for doing these things?" Jesus answered them, "Destroy this temple, and in three days I will raise it up." The Jews then said, "It has taken forty-six years to build this temple, and you will raise it up in three days?" But he was speaking about the temple of his body. When therefore he was raised from the dead, his disciples remembered that he had said this, and they believed the Scripture and the word that Jesus had spoken. (2.18–22)

Your day is in good hands when you entrust it to the God of the third day.

WEDNESDAY

Charm is Deceitful and Beauty is Vain, But...

Charm is deceitful, and beauty is vain,
  but a woman who fears the LORD is to be praised.
Give her of the fruit of her hands,
  and let her works praise her in the gates. (Prov 31.30–31)

God is the Creator of beauty, but he has warned us about building our lives, our senses of worth, and our relationships on beauty that will not last. The woman who woos a man with nothing more than physical charm and outward beauty is wooing on fleeting terms.

Charm is "deceitful" in that it is temporary. Youthful bodies age. Circumstances change. Interests evolve.

Beauty is "vain" in that it is superficial. There is an outward beauty that goes no deeper than the skin. But what about the inner woman? What about her heart—the mental, moral, and spiritual source that will come to shape the springs of her life (Prov 4.23)?

Tweens, teens, single ladies, and married women are absolutely bombarded in our secular culture with images of "real womanhood" founded on deceitful charm and vain beauty.

"But a woman who fears the LORD is to be praised." Youthful circumstances change, but reverence for God endures. Youthful bodies age, but Christlike character will cause the hidden person of the heart to thrive. Youthful interests evolve, but the works of a woman who loves the Lord are worthy of praise (Prov 31.31).

Parents, let's teach our daughters that the greatest role models aren't in Hollywood or the scroll of their social media feeds. True role models are those who fear the Lord.

Ladies, root your identity in God, not the vain deceptions of secular culture. Resolve that your physical beauty will serve as a complement to the imperishable beauty of a gentle, quiet, God-centered spirit (1 Pet 3.4). Let your service as a living sacrifice be the primary source of your praise (Rom 12.1).

Single men, guard against the intoxication of a forbidden woman who will lead you away from the Lord (Prov 5).

Married men, "an excellent wife who can find? She is far more precious than jewels. The heart of her husband trusts in her, and he will have no lack of gain" (Prov 31.10–11).

A woman who fears the Lord is to be praised. Be a source of that praise today.

THURSDAY

When Joy and Grief Are Next Door Neighbors

"Great persecution" in one city, "much joy" in another. I had never noticed how closely those very different experiences appear in Acts 8.

In Jerusalem, "a great persecution against the church" began on the day of Stephen's execution. "Saul was ravaging the church, and entering house after house, he dragged off men and women and committed them to prison" (8.1–3).

At the same time, Philip proclaims the Christ to a nearby city of Samaria.

> And the crowds with one accord paid attention to what was being said by Philip, when they heard him and saw the signs that he did. For unclean spirits, crying out with a loud voice, came out of many who had them, and many who were paralyzed or lame were healed. So there was much joy in that city. (8.6–8)

"Great persecution" and "much joy," separated by just six verses. Sometimes the extremes sit even closer. Less than six feet apart, one heart is broken, another is bursting at the seams with happiness. In the same pew, one is crying and another can't stop smiling. Social media feeds put the wide spectrum on full display, day after day—pain and gain, funerals and birth announcements, adversity and prosperity, setback and progress, devastating shocks and joyful surprises. Who is sufficient to celebrate and support (and personally cope) in this swirl of emotional whiplash?

Slow down long enough to realize what Luke is documenting for us in Acts 8, and notice where he's pointing. Christians in Jerusalem were being ravaged. What did they need? There was much joy a few miles down the road in Samaria. From where did it come and how would it be sustained? What could possibly be sufficient to help one group of people endure terrible suffering, while at the same time leading others to the heights of gladness?

The gospel of Jesus Christ.

Philip wasn't being insensitive to the heartache in Jerusalem when he went down and proclaimed good news to the city of Samaria. They needed Jesus. The apostles weren't being shortsighted when they stayed in Jerusalem to help others hold on through the hurricane of persecution. They needed Jesus.

The gospel of Christ is solid enough to support people on both extremes of the emotional spectrum. It's powerful enough to lead us to joy inexpressible and filled with glory, introducing us to the outcome of faith, the salvation of our souls. But it's also powerful enough to equip us with patience in tribulation, peace in uncertainty, and hope in grief.

Likewise, the body of Christ is big enough to support the highest highs and the lowest lows. What a sacred privilege to serve as the hands and feet of Jesus! We celebrate and comfort. Our tears spring from happiness and sadness. We lift the tired arms of someone today, only to have our own weak knees strengthened by someone else tomorrow. In humility we rejoice with those who are rejoicing, with compassion we weep with those who are weeping. By grace we've been blessed with the opportunity to serve as small parts of something so much larger than ourselves.

Who is sufficient when joy and grief are next door neighbors? Not me, and not you. But Jesus was in Acts 8, and he still is today.

FRIDAY

"But God Remembered Noah"

> In the six hundredth year of Noah's life, in the second month, on
> the seventeenth day of the month, on that day all the fountains of
> the great deep burst forth, and the windows of the heavens were
> opened. And rain fell upon the earth forty days and forty nights.
> (Gen 7.11–12)

Imagine the pitter-patter of the first rain drops on that giant vessel of gopher wood. What did it sound like from the inside as the windows of the heavens were opened? How did Noah, his wife, his three sons and their wives spend that first anxious night? Were they able to get a wink of sleep? What did it feel like and smell like and sound like as this ark full of livestock, creeping things, and birds began to be lifted from its construction site and carried upon the waters, high above the earth?

"All the high mountains under the whole heaven were covered." Everything on the dry land in whose nostrils was the breath of life died. Water would reign on the earth for the next five months.

How helpless must Noah have felt in that season?

Before all the fountains of the great deep began to burst, Noah couldn't stem the wickedness of mankind that was great on God's good earth. He couldn't keep the thoughts of human hearts from being only evil continually. He couldn't close his eyes, snap his fingers, and wish man-made corruption away.

But Noah could walk with God. He could choose to believe the Lord's warnings concerning events as yet unseen. By faith he could follow God's directions and build with reverent fear. He could shine as a light in the darkness. He could resolve to stand up and stand out, unashamed.

Before all the windows of the heavens began to open, Noah couldn't make people listen. He couldn't force them into safety. Over the course of decades, he was unable to convince the over-whelming majority that God meant what he had said.

Noah couldn't keep the rain from falling. Once it started, he couldn't make it stop. The vessel carrying him had no rudder, no sails to adjust, no helm from which to steer. When the Lord "shut him in," Noah had no idea how long this terrible journey would last. He and his family would spend just over a year in that ark.

But God remembered Noah… (8.1)

There was a flood of things Noah couldn't do, couldn't stop, couldn't understand. But Noah walked with God. He believed God. He trusted God. He did all that God commanded him.

And God remembered Noah.

As we head into this weekend, there's a flood of things we can't do. Frustrating things we can't control or stop. Broken things we can't fix. Perplexing things we struggle to understand. Things we wish just weren't so.

But we can walk with God. We can believe God. We can trust God. We can do what God has commanded us to do. And if we walk by this faith? The same God who remembered Noah will not forget or misplace us.

SATURDAY

The Powerful Present Tense

Now the point in what we are saying is this… (Heb 8.1a)

The Letter to the Hebrews was written nearly 2,000 years ago. That's an **old** letter. But notice the power of the present tense.

> …we **have** such a high priest, one who **is** seated at the right hand of the throne of the Majesty in heaven, a minister in the holy places, in the true tent that the Lord set up, not man. (8.1b-2)

> But as it is, Christ has obtained a ministry that is as much more excellent than the old as the covenant he **mediates** is better, since it is enacted on better promises. (8.6)

We don't simply study the life and teachings of a man who lived a long, long time ago. This morning, we **have**—*present tense*—a high priest who is able to sympathize with our weaknesses.

We don't hope against hope that someone will eventually discover some way to atone for our sins and somehow reconcile us to our holy Creator. This afternoon, he **mediates**—*present tense*—on behalf of his brothers and sisters, inviting us to draw near with confidence to the throne of grace in his name.

We've not been left in the dark as to how our story ends, vainly wishing upon a cold, unresponsive star that good will someday triumph over evil. This evening, our King **is seated**—*present tense*—at the throne of the Majesty in heaven.

God's people unashamedly read very old letters. Why? Because what was true 2,000 years ago is just as current as the latest breaking news. Those ancient letters, breathed out by God, are **living** and **active** (4.12). Christians have been born again to a **living** hope (1 Pet 1.3), not of perishable seed but of imperishable, through the **living** and **abiding** word of God (1 Pet 1.23).

He mediates. We have. He reigns. The powerful present tense.

WEEK SIX

SUNDAY

"From God to the Road"

My wife Shelly used to babysit a little boy named Dustin who would tell her every once in a while that he loved her "from God to the road." That was just about as big and wide as Dustin could imagine at 3 years old. "From God to the road."

In Psalm 36, David seems to be similarly stretching for words to describe the wonder of our matchless Creator.

> Your steadfast love, O LORD, extends to the heavens,
> your faithfulness to the clouds.
> Your righteousness is like the mountains of God;
> your judgments are like the great deep... (36.5–6)

Recognizing these truths led David to worship, and the next few lines of Psalm 36 continue to serve as a fountain of living fuel for our own worship today.

> How precious is your steadfast love, O God!
> The children of mankind take refuge in the shadow of your wings.
> They feast on the abundance of your house,
> and you give them drink from the river of your delights.
> For with you is the fountain of life;
> in your light do we see light.
> Oh, continue your steadfast love to those who know you,
> and your righteousness to the upright of heart! (36.7–10)

What wonderful words to **savor** as we offer our own sacrifice of praise today…

Precious. How precious is the LORD's *steadfast* love!

Refuge. In the shadow of his wings, what do we really have to fear?

Abundance. Our Father in heaven is the eager, gracious giver of every good and perfect gift.

Delight. He is the overflowing, never-ending source of an entire *river* of delights.

Incredible blessings that continue to stretch from God to the road.

MONDAY

Tell Me the Truth

In 2 Chronicles 18, King Jehoshaphat, whose heart "was coura-geous in the ways of the LORD" (17.6), made a near-fatal mistake. "He made a marriage alliance with Ahab," king of Israel (18.1). After some years, Ahab proposed a joint war effort to recapture Ramoth-gilead from the Syrians. Jehoshaphat's only request? "In-quire first for the word of the LORD."

Ahab easily gathered 400 prophets who would tell him exactly what he wanted to hear: "Go up, for God will give it into the hand of the king." Jehoshaphat wisely inquired, "Is there not here an-other prophet of the LORD of whom we may inquire?" Jehoshaphat wanted to hear from Yahweh. Finally, the king of Israel reluctantly acknowledged, "There is yet one man by whom we may inquire of the LORD, Micaiah the son of Imlah; but I hate him, for he never prophesies good concerning me, but always evil" (18.7).

What a window into Ahab's heart! Michaiah never told Ahab what he wanted to hear. It was always rebukes, corrections, and calls for repentance from Michaiah (and if you know anything about Ahab, you know why). Even the thought of Michaiah grated on Ahab's nerves. "I hate him," the king straightforwardly revealed.

Jehoshaphat eventually compelled Ahab to send for Michaiah.

And the messenger who went to summon Micaiah said to him, "Behold, the words of the prophets with one accord are favorable to the king. Let your word be like the word of one of them, and speak favorably." But Micaiah said, "As the LORD lives, what my God says, that I will speak." (18.12–13)

Here's a point worth thinking about this week: do the people in my life have permission to tell me what I need to hear? Is my heart humble enough to consistently give them the green light to say what needs to be said? Have my past actions and reactions demonstrated a willingness to respond to the truth, even when it steps on my toes? Have I shown a real desire to become more like Jesus, whatever the cost? To keep in step with the Spirit? To be the best version of me I can possibly be?

Husbands and wives, we all have blind spots. Let's love each other enough to tell and hear the truth about ourselves.

Fathers and mothers, our children are works in progress. Let's love them enough to bring them up in the discipline and instruction of the Lord (Eph 6.4). Let's remember that sometimes, the most powerful teaching moments are when *we* are willing to acknowledge our own shortcomings to them.

Let's be thankful for preachers and teachers who love us enough to preach the word, reproving, rebuking, and exhorting us with complete patience and teaching (2 Tim 4.2).

Let's obey our shepherds and submit to them, for they are keeping watch over our souls, as those who will have to give an account. Let them do this with joy and not with groaning, for that would be of no advantage to us (Heb 13.17).

How thankful we ought to be for brothers and sisters in Christ who care enough to admonish us when we are idle, encourage us when we are fainthearted, and help us when we are weak (1 Thes 5.14).

Ahab's heart had grown so hard that he hated Michaiah for telling him the truth. **Want something bold to pray this week?** Let's pray for people who love us enough to tell us the truth. Then, before we say "Amen," let's pray for the wisdom to be quick to hear, slow to speak, and slow to anger; "for the anger of man does not produce the righteousness of God" (James 1.19–20).

TUESDAY

Love Incorruptible in an All-Too-Corruptible World

> Peace be to the brothers and sisters, and love with faith, from God the Father and the Lord Jesus Christ. Grace be with all who love our Lord Jesus Christ with **love incorruptible**. (Eph 6.23–24)

So concludes Paul's letter to the Ephesians. Take a moment to turn those God-breathed words over in your mind today. If something is "corruptible," it's perishable. Corruptible things are temporary things. Those flowers you plant in the Spring? Corruptible. Those pumpkins you put on your front porch in the Fall? Corruptible. The milk in your refrigerator right now? Slowly perishing inside a corruptible jug stamped with a perishable date on the side.

Want an interesting challenge? Take mental notes throughout the day of how many things around you are corruptible. So much of what grabs our attention and consumes our focus is merely temporary. Houses. Cars. Digital gadgets. Degrees. Careers. Social media. Hobbies. Sports. Clothes. Even our own bodies are "perishable" (1 Cor 15.42).

But do you know what's within your grasp today that is truly **"incorruptible"**? Love. Love "from God the Father and the Lord Jesus Christ" is a major focal point in *Ephesians*.

> **In love** he predestined us for adoption as sons through Jesus Christ… (1.4–5)

> But God, being rich in mercy, because of **the great love with which he loved us**, even when we were dead in our trespasses,

made us alive together with Christ—by grace you have been saved... (2.4–5)

...so that Christ may dwell in your hearts through faith—that you, being **rooted and grounded in love**, may have strength to comprehend with all the saints what is the breadth and length and height and depth, and to know **the love of Christ that surpasses knowledge**, that you may be filled with all the fullness of God. (3.17–19)

God loved us first. That's why Paul is able to conclude his letter with, "Peace be to the brothers and sisters, and love with faith, from God the Father and the Lord Jesus Christ." But don't rush by his last sentence...

Grace be with all who love our Lord Jesus Christ with love incorruptible.

The infinite, eternal God may have loved us first, but his isn't the only love that can endure, "incorruptible." In an all-too-temporary world, with the conclusion of a 2,000-year-old letter, we're being pointed to what really lasts. Beyond the wasting away of our outer selves. Beyond trials. Beyond grief. Beyond death itself ... is love—**incorruptible** love for our Lord Jesus Christ. Do you realize what that means? Your house won't stand forever. Your car will rust. Your digital toys will break. Your education opens brief opportunities. Your career is temporary. Fame is fleeting. Your body is growing older. To draw our significance and rest our hope in any of those things is vanity and folly. But love for Jesus endures. Loving the Lord your God with all your heart, soul, mind, and strength doesn't pass away. Earthbound "love with faith" echoes in eternity.

So here's an aim worthy of this God-given week: to think of the temporary things around you as truly *temporary* and to prioritize "love incorruptible" above everything else. That's life the way our heavenly Father intended it to be.

WEDNESDAY

Respecting God Enough to Wait

It was a big deal. The first anniversary of the Passover. The original event had taken place in Egypt in conjunction with the tenth plague. The blood of unblemished lambs had been applied to the lintels and doorposts of houses. "When I see the blood," the LORD had promised, "I will pass over you" (Exo 12.13).

> All the people of Israel did just as the LORD commanded Moses and Aaron. And on that very day the LORD brought the people of Israel out of the land of Egypt by their hosts. (12.50–51)

Before the blood was even shed, God had commanded, "You shall observe this day, throughout your generations, as a statue forever. In the first month, from the fourteenth day of the month at evening…" (12.17–18)

And an entire year had passed. Hundreds of thousands of Israelites were in the wilderness of Sinai on the fourteenth day of the first month. "And they kept the Passover… according to all that the LORD commanded Moses, so the people of Israel did" (Num 9.5). But Numbers 9 goes on to describe an interesting scenario.

> And there were certain men who were unclean through touching a dead body, so that they could not keep the Passover on that day, and they came before Moses and Aaron on that day. And those men said to him, "We are unclean through touching a dead body. Why are we kept from bringing the LORD's offering at its appointed time among the people of Israel?" (9.6–7)

Tough question. Good question. Notice Moses' humble, wise response:

"Wait, that I may hear what the LORD will command concerning you." (9.8)

Thousands of years later, isn't that a wise principle we should remember and apply? When we or others find it very easy and natural to say…

- "Why can't we?"
- "I think God would be okay with this."
- "In fact, I think God would like this."
- "Why should we be left out?"
- "We have a good reason."
- "I think we should be able to…"
- "Why shouldn't we?"
- "Wouldn't it make good sense to…"
- "We're excited to try…"
- "I think it would be best to…"
- "As long as we're zealous and sincere…"

…there's still much we can learn from Moses' wise, restrained reasoning. "Wait. Before we act or assume or presume, we need to consult the word of God."

Just because I *can* doesn't mean I should. *I* may think it makes perfectly good sense, but that doesn't automatically mean my Creator agrees. My eagerness, enthusiasm, and sincerity isn't a license to do whatever I want. As it turns out, the LORD had something to say about the matter (Num 9.9–14), and it probably wasn't what those unclean men or Moses would have guessed. What if Moses had just assumed what God thought or presumed he had the right to answer the question on his own?

If a servant of the LORD with the stature of Moses realized the authority of the Almighty needed to be consulted and respected, shouldn't I?

THURSDAY

The Comforted Comforters

Grace to you and peace from God our Father and the Lord Jesus
Christ.

Blessed be the God and Father of our Lord Jesus Christ, the
Father of mercies and God of all comfort... (2 Cor 1.2–3)

As today's Bible reading meandered into 2 Corinthians 1 and I
read Paul's greeting, I had a flashback and vague recollection of
something I might have written a long time ago. After finishing
the chapter, I did a little digging and found these paragraphs from
July 2008. There's not a lot buried that deep in the archives worth
dusting off and revisiting, but this simple reflection was an encouraging reminder for me today. Maybe it will help you too.

❋ ❋ ❋ ❋ ❋

Shelly and I have been blessed with three beautiful daughters.
Chloe is seven, Jadyn is two, and Emma is almost four months old.
Life together is nearly always noisy, typically chaotic, but abundantly blessed. As odd as it may sound, I think one of my favorite
memories will be of crying from the backseat of the car.

Chloe is Shelly's little righthand assistant, an amazing helper
with her little sisters. It really bothers her when one of them is up-
set, especially if they're buckled down tight in a car seat. From the
days that Jadyn was an infant, Chloe picked up on her mother's
habit of singing "Jesus Loves Me" or "Can You Count the Stars?"
If Jadyn cried, Chloe would almost instinctively start singing.

Now Emma is the infant. She *really* doesn't like her car seat and I can assure you there's absolutely nothing wrong with her lungs or tear ducts. But what a special moment it was today when Jadyn, all on her own, began singing "Jesus Loves Me" to Emma in her distinctive two-year-old voice. The comforted had learned from her older sister to serve as comforter to her younger sister.

As the simple lyrics of "Jesus Loves Me" became the oft-repeated soundtrack for yet another distressing car ride, I thought of Paul's encouragement in his second letter to the church at Corinth:

> Blessed be the God and Father of our Lord Jesus Christ, the Father of mercies and God of all comfort, who comforts us in all our affliction, so that we may be able to comfort those who are in any affliction, with the comfort with which we ourselves are comforted by God. (1.3–4)

The two-year-old singing on the right side of the backseat had no idea how long the journey would last, but she can sing. The seven-year-old on the left side of the backseat couldn't take the wheel or reach the pedals, but she knows how to comfort. She learned from Shelly, who learned from her own mother, years before. Our little car was full of comforted comforters.

"Blessed be the God of all comfort." Don't just read over that. Meditate on this powerful description: "God of all comfort." Carry it with you today. Through many sorrows, trials, and afflictions, he has comforted us. Let's not be reservoirs; let's be channels. Let's recognize and give thanks for our blessings, and then let's *be* blessed blessings to the people around us. How graciously and patiently we've been comforted! In turn, let's serve as selfless links in a long chain of comforted comforters.

Jesus, take this heart of mine,
    Make it pure and wholly Thine;
Thou hast bled and died for me;
    I will henceforth live for Thee. (Anna B. Warner, 1860)

FRIDAY

A Fishhook Lodged In My Eye

It's hard for me to imagine something more unpleasant than having a fishhook lodged in my eye.

In Numbers 33, Israel's journey from Egyptian slavery to the doorstep of the Promised Land is recounted.

> These are the stages of the people of Israel, when they went out of the land of Egypt by their companies under the leadership of Moses and Aaron. Moses wrote down their starting places, stage by stage, by command of the LORD, and these are their stages according to their starting places... (33.1–2)

Moses documents forty long years' worth of starts and stops... Rameses... Succoth... Marah... Elim... the Red Sea... Rephidim... Sinai... Nebo... Moab... and many, many places in between. The children of Israel were closer now to their new God-given home than ever before.

> And the LORD spoke to Moses in the plains of Moab by the Jordan at Jericho, saying, "Speak to the people of Israel and say to them, When you pass over the Jordan into the land of Canaan, then you shall drive out all the inhabitants of the land from before you and destroy all their figured stones and destroy all their metal images and demolish all their high places. And you shall take possession of the land and settle in it, for I have given the land to you to possess it... But if you do not drive out the inhabitants of the land from before you, then those of them whom you let

remain shall be as barbs in your eyes and thorns in your sides, and they shall trouble you in the land where you dwell." (33.50–53, 55)

The inhabitants of this land were idolatrous, immoral, ungodly people. To settle among them, tolerate their ways of life, and adapt to their practices would have devastating consequences. Imagine, God warns, barbs in your eyes and thorns in your sides—that's what you can expect if you cozy up next to sin.

We live in a different time, under different circumstances, as citizens of a very different kingdom, but the painful analogy is still worth thinking about. The call to wage war on the battlefield of our own hearts is no less urgent. Listen to Colossians 3.5–9:

> Put to death therefore what is earthly in you: sexual immorality, impurity, passion, evil desire, and covetousness, which is idolatry. On account of these the wrath of God is coming. In these you too once walked, when you were living in them. But now you must put them all away: anger, wrath, malice, slander, and obscene talk from your mouth. Do not lie to one another, seeing that you have put off the old self with its practices…

Put sin to death. Wake up and realize that impure gazes are like barbed wire in your eyes. Covetousness is like a branch of thorns lodged in your ribs. Wrath and malice are poisons. Don't flirt with sexual immorality. Don't set up camp in the territory of evil desire. Don't surrender to slander, or rationalize obscene talk, or build your home with lies. Drive those things out of the territory of your heart. Put to death what is earthly in you.

> Let no one say when he is tempted, "I am being tempted by God," for God cannot be tempted with evil, and he himself tempts no one. But each person is tempted when he is lured and enticed by his own desire. (James 1.13–14)

Sin makes promises. It feels good for a little while. It slows us down, encourages us to settle, selling at a bargain the illusion that we're in control. We can leave, we're led to believe, unhindered and unaffected whenever we want. In fact, it might be worth sacrificing everything to just stay right where we are, in forbidden territory. After all, will it really turn out to be that big of a deal?

The next time I'm tempted to think like that, I need to remember how incredibly unpleasant it would be to have a fishhook lodged in my eye.

SATURDAY

His Commandments Are Not Burdensome

For this is the love of God, that we keep his commandments. And his commandments are not burdensome. (1 John 5.3)

That's a truth worth meditating upon throughout the day. My Creator's commandments are not burdensome. His heart is not set on weighing me down. His aim is not to keep me *from* anything that is good *for* me. He has revealed his commandments *to* us because he is *for* us. Far from being a loathsome burden, his commandments are expressions of his perfect love and holy concern for his image-bearers.

"You shall have no other gods before me." Far from burdensome, it's what we need to hear as his creation.

"You shall not make for yourself a carved image." Far from burdensome, it's a guardrail to keep us from self-centered foolishness.

"Honor your father and your mother." Far from burdensome, it's a foundational stepping stone to learning respect for authority.

"You shall not murder." Far from burdensome, it's fundamental to human flourishing.

"You shall not commit adultery." Far from burdensome, it's a hedge to protect the most intimate relationship we can enjoy with another human being.

"You shall not steal." Far from burdensome, it's one of the most easily understood applications of the Golden Rule.

"You shall love the Lord your God with all your heart, soul, mind, and strength." Far from burdensome, it's the great and first commandment of the God who loves us enough to send his only Son to rescue us.

"You shall love your neighbor as yourself." Far from burdensome, it's a supporting beam of the Law and the Prophets that served as a tutor to lead us to our Savior.

On and on and on, examples could be given to verify this truth: my Creator's commandments are not burdensome. He warns because he cares. He exhorts because he cherishes. He commands because he loves.

Having been loved *first*, may we walk in the light of this truth today:

> For this is the love of God, that we keep his commandments. And his commandments are not burdensome.

WEEK SEVEN

SUNDAY

The Shelter and the Shadow

He who dwells in the shelter of the Most High
    will abide in the shadow of the Almighty. (Psa 91.1)

Shelter is good, but shelter coupled with the shadow of the Builder is better.

Think of shelter as provision. A shelter provides overnight refuge to the weary hiker on the Appalachian Trail. A fortress provides protective shelter to people who can't defend themselves. Shelter is good. Our homes are to be shelters for our children. But what if a husband and father who has worked to provide shelter—a roof over the heads of his wife and children—decides to abandon his family? Shelter is good, but shelter coupled with the shadow of the builder is better.

If shelter is provision, think of shadow as presence. An absent father casts no shadow over his son or daughter. My shadow will not be seen where I am not present. Sadly, not all who *are* present to cast a shadow are shelters to the people around them. Too often, the presence of some is more like a storm that batters and erodes the hearts of those who need them most. Devastating harm can be left in the wake of their imposing shadow.

This is what makes Psalm 91 so precious. The same God who casts an unequaled shadow has the gracious desire to shelter his people. He is the perfect Provider who is powerfully present. "He will cover you with his pinions, and under his wings you will find refuge" (91.4). Of the man or woman who abides in his shadow, this Builder promises:

> "Because he holds fast to me in love, I will deliver him;
>> I will protect him, because he knows my name." (91.14)

I live in a house built by someone whose name I don't know. I drive a car engineered by someone whose name I don't know. I cross bridges designed by architects whose names I don't know. But my Creator? His name I know. He is the Most High who has provided the shelter of my salvation. He is the Almighty who daily casts the shadow in which I was created to abide. Therefore…

> I will say to the LORD, "My refuge and my fortress,
>> my God, in whom I trust." (91.2)

Shelter and shadow. Provision and presence. Shelter is good, but when those in need of refuge are able to trust and abide in the very shadow of the gracious Builder? That's the blessed best.

MONDAY

Whoever Walks With the Wise Becomes Wise

Whoever walks with the wise becomes wise, but the companion of fools will suffer harm. (Prov 13.20)

Do you want to grow in wisdom? "Walk" with the wise this week.

- Read what wise people have written.
- Listen to what wise people say, preach, and teach.
- Fill your social media streams with posts from wise people.
- Show hospitality to wise people that you might get to know them better.
- Ask to get involved with wise people as they serve others.
- When a wise person offers advice, correction, or a rebuke, listen intently.

"Walk" with the sort of people God would describe as "wise" and it will shape you for the better.

Do you want to increase in foolishness? "Walk" with fools.

- Read what foolish people have written.
- Listen to what foolish people say, preach, and teach.
- Fill your social media streams with posts from foolish people.
- Spend free time with foolish people who want to do foolish things.
- Follow the lead of foolish people who are only looking out for themselves.

- When a wise person offers advice, correction, or a rebuke, don't listen.

"Walk" with the sort of people God describes as "fools" and it will harm you. God has warned you because he loves you.

So, with whom will you "walk" this week?

TUESDAY

The Family Story

If you want to know Jesus, you should gradually learn his family story.

That's what happens when we get to know each other today. Over the course of time and several conversations, we learn each other's family stories. Where are you from? To whom are you related? Where have you lived? Where did you go to school? How did you meet? How did you get here? What common connections do we have?

In Romans 9.4–5, Paul summarizes Jesus' family story.

> They are Israelites, and to them belong the adoption, the glory, the covenants, the giving of the law, the worship, and the promises. To them belong the patriarchs, and from their race, according to the flesh, is the Christ, who is God over all, blessed forever. Amen.

Jesus' family are the descendants of the patriarchs—Abraham, Isaac, and Jacob. They are God's adopted people. They beheld his glory firsthand in their deliverance from Egyptian slavery. They entered into a covenant with him and received his law at Mount Sinai. God dwelt among them in the tabernacle and eventually the temple. He made precious and very great promises to them. Most precious of all? Through their family line came Jesus the Christ, Immanuel, God with us, who is blessed forever and willing to be a blessing to every human being.

It's tough reading here and there, but every time you open your Bible to the Old Testament, you're entering into the conversation. Learn the family story and you come to know Jesus all the better. But even more, you find **your** place in the greatest story ever told.

WEDNESDAY

"What Do Those Stones Mean to You?"

After decades of wandering in the wilderness, the children of Israel had finally stepped foot in the Promised Land.

> When all the nation had finished passing over the Jordan, the LORD said to Joshua, "Take twelve men from the people, from each tribe a man, and command them, saying, 'Take twelve stones from here out of the midst of the Jordan, from the very place where the priests' feet stood firmly, and bring them over with you and lay them down in the place where you lodge tonight.'" Then Joshua called the twelve men from the people of Israel, whom he had appointed, a man from each tribe. And Joshua said to them, "Pass on before the ark of the LORD your God into the midst of the Jordan, and take up each of you a stone upon his shoulder, according to the number of the tribes of the people of Israel, that this may be a sign among you. When your children ask in time to come, '**What do those stones mean to you?**' then you shall tell them that the waters of the Jordan were cut off before the ark of the covenant of the LORD. When it passed over the Jordan, the waters of the Jordan were cut off. So these stones shall be to the people of Israel a memorial forever." (Josh 4.1–7)

"What do those stones mean to you?" So much more than a meaningless pile of riverbed rocks, this was to be a marker for the descendants of Abraham, a reminder of an incredible event in their history. But historical markers are easily passed by and taken for granted, aren't they? Even more than a monument to the past, this collection of stones was intended to provide a teaching opportunity for the present, generation after generation.

> "When your children ask their fathers in times to come, '**What do those stones mean?**' then you shall let your children know, 'Israel passed over this Jordan on dry ground.' For the LORD your God dried up the waters of the Jordan for you until you passed over, as the LORD your God did to the Red Sea, which he dried up for us until we passed over, so that all the peoples of the earth may know that the hand of the LORD is mighty, that you may fear the LORD your God forever." (4.22–24)

Those stones were a connection to the past, providing a teaching opportunity in the present, that generations to come might know and fear and build a relationship with the LORD their God.

Do you realize that *we* have similar teaching opportunities on the first day of every week? We may not stand with our children, grandchildren, or the children of our church family on the banks of the Jordan River looking at twelve literal stones, but the questions continue to arise, and each one of us provides an answer of our own.

- "What does that Bible mean to you?"
- "What do these hymns mean to you?"
- "What does prayer mean to you?"
- "What does this unleavened bread and fruit of the vine mean to you?"
- "What does the preaching of God's word mean to you?"
- "What does the Savior's invitation mean to you?"
- "What does the opportunity to sacrifice for the Lord and the work of his kingdom mean to you?"

With my priorities, my attitude, and my engagement, what answers am I giving?

Do you realize that those opportunities don't just bubble to the surface every Sunday morning? Whether we look at them as opportunities or not, we're providing life-altering answers to eternity-shaping questions, day after day after day.

- "What does marriage mean to you?"
- "What do your brothers and sisters in Christ mean to you?"
- "What does hospitality mean to you?"
- "What does patience mean to you?"
- "What does forgiveness mean to you?"
- "What does love mean to you?"
- "What do the poor, the hurting, and the lost mean to you?"

By my actions, interactions, and reactions, what answers am I giving?

Those twelve stones were so much more than a marker of an incredible moment in history. They provided an ongoing opportunity to teach the next generation, "Here is what those stones mean to me. Let me tell you what they ought to mean to you."

Take the time to look around today. Little (and not so little) eyes, ears, and hearts are constantly noticing, learning, asking questions, and soaking up impressions. **"What does** _____ **mean to you?"** Be humbled by the fact that you've already given countless answers. Ready or not, you'll continue to give answers.

Does the answer you'd *like* to give harmonize with the answer you're actually giving? If not, what needs to change?

Let's live in such a way that all the peoples of the earth may know. The hand of the Lord is mighty. He is worthy of our fearful service. Today and forever.

THURSDAY

"What Is This?"

It's good for us to periodically ask a fundamental question when we pick up our Bibles—"What is this?" As I read this book, *what* am I reading? Is this simply someone else's mail? Just an old record of things that happened a really long time ago? Are these the claims of someone who witnessed extraordinary things, but things that don't really relate to me? What *is* this big old book, and how could it possibly be worthy of my attention and application after 2,000 years?

Acts 28 stands as a simple signpost at the crossroads of those good questions. What it continues to reveal is worth reflecting upon today.

The apostle Paul had carried the gospel all the way to Rome. He was able to spend a couple of years welcoming all who came to him, proclaiming the kingdom of God and teaching about the Lord Jesus Christ with all boldness (28.30–31). On one occasion, the local leaders of the Jews appointed a day to hear Paul out.

> From morning till evening, he expounded to them, testifying to the kingdom of God and trying to convince them about Jesus both from the Law of Moses and from the Prophets. And some were convinced by what he said, but others disbelieved. And disagreeing among themselves, they departed after Paul had made one statement... (28.23–25)

In this moment, it's as if Luke—our narrator—pauses, looks us in the eye, lowers his voice, and encourages us to lean in a little closer. He wants to make sure we're listening intently. "Don't miss this. What Paul said next is truly significant." So let's follow Luke's leading. Of all the things Paul said "from morning till evening" that day, and of all the things Luke could have recorded, he gave us this "one statement":

> "The Holy Spirit was right in saying to your fathers through Isaiah the prophet:
>
>> 'Go to this people, and say,
>> "You will indeed hear but never understand,
>>   and you will indeed see but never perceive."
>> For this people's heart has grown dull,
>>   and with their ears they can barely hear,
>>   and their eyes they have closed;
>> lest they should see with their eyes
>>   and hear with their ears
>> and understand with their heart
>>   and turn, and I would heal them.'
>
> Therefore let it be known to you that this salvation of God has been sent to the Gentiles; they will listen." (28.25–28)

There's some foreboding news in those lines, but look again at the opening words of Paul's "one statement."

> "The Holy Spirit was right in saying to your fathers through Isaiah the prophet…"

Do you see the dots that are being connected? "The Holy Spirit said something to your forefathers seven centuries ago." We know that passage as Isaiah 6.9–10. "What the Holy Spirit said? He was right. It was true. But it wasn't just true of them. It's true of you. Those words may have been spoken through God's prophet 700 years ago, but they endure as a relevant reflection of you. Today."

What we've just been shown is extraordinary! Via Luke through Paul through Isaiah through the Holy Spirit there's a direct connection from the Scriptures of the past to the hearts of people in the present. Think about that...

For us, for me—in the twenty-first century—it's easy to reach the end of a historical book like *Acts*, read the closing verses, shut the book, and move on without realizing the awesome significance of what I'm holding in my hands. "What is this?" As I read this big old book, *what* am I reading? Let's allow Luke to continue to connect the dots for us today...

"The Holy Spirit said extraordinary things a long time ago. He captured history, revealed prophecies, conveyed serious warnings, and delivered great promises of assurance and hope. What he said was right. It was true, and it continues to be true, *of* you and *for* you. A direct, unbroken connection continues to live from the Scriptures of the past to the hearts of people in the present. Therefore let it be known to you..."

That's the posture we ought to have as we open our Bibles. "Let it be known to you." This is the revelation of my Creator. These are the words of my King. This is light for my path provided by the Holy Spirit of God."

Some were convinced that day in Rome. Others disbelieved. The same is still unfolding 2,000 years later. For all who will listen, the salvation of God continues to be extended.

So let's listen carefully and eagerly.

FRIDAY

"Ask What I Shall Give You"

> At Gibeon the LORD appeared to Solomon in a dream by night, and God said, "Ask what I shall give you." (1 Kings 3.5)

What an incredible invitation! Can you imagine? This isn't a fictional genie in a bottle. This is the Lord of heaven and earth asking *you*, "What do you want me to give you?" How would you have responded if you were in Solomon's royal sandals?

There's a lot we can learn and plenty of seeds for prayer we can pick up and adopt from the way Solomon responds. If I could very loosely paraphrase the next few verses…

O LORD my God, you have shown great and steadfast love to your servants in the past.

You have recognized when your servants have walked before you in faithfulness, righteousness, and uprightness of heart toward you.

You have been faithful in great and steadfast love. You continue to be the giver of great and undeserved gifts to your people. Though I am undeserving of the gifts you have already given me, you have brought me this far. You have been so very gracious to me.

I am in need.

There is so much I do not know.

There are so many paths I have not traveled.

Great challenges and obstacles lie ahead of me and I do not know the way. I am inadequate on my own to meet the challenges and walk the path.

Therefore, O LORD my God, I humbly ask for wisdom. Please give me an understanding mind that I might know you and your will. Help me grow in my ability to distinguish right from wrong, good from evil, wise from foolish, and worthwhile from wasteful. Shape me, O LORD my God, into the right influence on others, for your name's sake.

I love you, LORD, and I am your servant.

What an incredible prayer! And how did the LORD respond?

"Behold, I now do according to your word. Behold, I give you a wise and discerning mind, so that none like you has been before you and none like you shall arise after you." (3.12)

To this day, we continue to be impressed at many of Solomon's accomplishments and seek to apply the written fruits of his God-given wisdom. But do you realize and appreciate that someone "greater than Solomon" (Matt 12.42) eventually stepped onto the scene and extended another invitation—not solely to a king in a bygone era, but to anyone willing to follow him at any point in history?

"Ask, and it will be given to you; seek, and you will find; knock, and it will be opened to you. For everyone who asks receives, and the one who seeks finds, and to the one who knocks it will be opened. Or which one of you, if his son asks him for bread, will give him a stone? Or if he asks for a fish, will give him a serpent? If you then, who are evil, know how to give good gifts to your children, how much more will your Father who is in heaven give good things to those who ask him!" (Matt 7.7–11)

What an incredible invitation! What if *I* prayed today to the God who heard Solomon? What if I prayed with the same humility? What if I prayerfully presented myself before heaven's throne with the heart of a servant, taking my Lord's invitation seriously? What sort of things could I pray for?

- "Give your servant an understanding mind" (James 1.5)
- "Give your servant a compassionate heart" (Luke 10.33)
- "Give your servant a focus on the 'one necessary thing'" (Luke 10.41–42)
- "Give your servant a forgiving spirit" (Matt 6.14–15)
- "Give your servant an evangelistic will" (Luke 10.2)
- "Give your servant peace that surpasses all understanding" (Phil 4.7)
- "Give your servant joy in you that is inexpressible and filled with glory" (1 Pet 1.8)
- "Give your servant the outcome of faith in you, salvation of the soul" (1 Pet 1.9)

You're not Solomon, but the One who is greater than Solomon has opened the door, extended the access, secured the intercession, and offered the invitation.

Ask. Seek. Knock.

Trust the heart of your Father in heaven who knows how to give good things to those who ask him.

SATURDAY

"What Is That to You? You Follow Me!"

In John 21, Jesus delivers some difficult news about Peter's future. In response…

> Peter turned and saw the disciple whom Jesus loved following them, the one who also had leaned back against him during the supper and had said, "Lord, who is it that is going to betray you?" When Peter saw him, he said to Jesus, "Lord, what about this man?" Jesus said to him, "If it is my will that he remain until I come, what is that to you? You follow me!" (21.20–22)

The circumstances are most certainly different, but the principle remains the same.

- Lord, some people have more talent than I do. **"What is that to you? You follow me!"**
- Lord, I had a reason to strike back; look at how she treated me. **"What is that to you? You follow me!"**
- Lord, that family has more stuff than we do. **"What is that to you? You follow me!"**
- Lord, I don't have the education he does. **"What is that to you? You follow me!"**

There is only one *you*. You're not someone else. You can't be. Others have different experiences, advantages, and challenges. But the principle remains the same: **"What is that to you? You follow me!"**

No one can follow Jesus *for* you. If you follow him, it's because *you've* made the choice to follow. And once that choice has been made, it doesn't really matter what other people have or do or say. **"What is that to me? I'm following Jesus!"**

Whomever we are, wherever we are, let's make and stand by that decision to follow him today.

WEEK EIGHT

SUNDAY

The Psalm 33 Trail

Could I invite you to hike the Psalm 33 trail with me today? If you give it a little bit of your time and lend some thought to its signs along the way, it will do you good. Promise.

The Psalm 33 trail leads us to overlooks and peaks high above much of the fog that clouds our vision. From its heights, a few of the valleys and switchbacks of life are put into far-reaching perspective. It's a 3,000-year-old trail, but it continues to provide much-needed fresh air to all who are willing to follow its leading.

A simple sign stands at the trailhead, setting the tone for the rest of our trek:

The earth is full of the steadfast love of the LORD. (33.5)

Look around today. Be intentional. Notice. Don't settle for the mundane. Work your way past the vain. Scavenge for the good stuff. Where can you see traces of your Creator's steadfast love? Turn down the artificial noise. Step away from the man-made distractions. See with fresh eyes. Listen with undistracted ears. The earth on which you live is **FULL** of the steadfast love of the LORD. As you soak that thought in today, realize…

By the word of the LORD the heavens were made,
 and by the breath of his mouth all their host. (33.6)

You have a Creator. Evidences of his invisible attributes—his eternal power and divine nature—surround you. Look up. Look down. Look around, in every direction, at the incredible, glorious things he has made.

> For he spoke, and it came to be;
> > he commanded, and it stood firm. (33.9)

As we perceive who he is with fresh eyes and understand with full hearts what he has done, why wouldn't we honor him as God? How could we fail to give him the thanks he is due?

> Let all the earth fear the LORD;
> > let all the inhabitants of the world stand in awe of him! (33.8)

Not everyone does, obviously. We live in a world where many claim to be wise apart from their Creator. Some exchange the glory of the immortal God for cheap imitations of their own making. We all experience, day by day, the ripple effects of living in a fallen world full of futile thinking—the rotten fruit of foolish, darkened hearts. But human selfishness and rebellion will never change God's nature, frustrate his plans, or overpower his eternal purposes.

> The LORD brings the counsel of the nations to nothing;
> > he frustrates the plans of the peoples.
> The counsel of the LORD stands forever,
> > the plans of his heart to all generations. (33.10–11)

What a blessing to hold in our hands the treasure chest of his written revelation to mankind! The plans of his heart and expressions of his will. His explanation of life, the way it was meant to be. Thousands of years' worth of history, preserved for our learning. The landscape of his work to save mankind, on full display. Priceless wisdom. Comforting promises. Fulfilled prophecies. Sacred writings. God-breathed Scripture. A lamp to our feet and a light to our path.

For the word of the LORD is upright,
and all his work is done in faithfulness.
He loves righteousness and justice. (33.4–5)

And he continues to teach us. Even on this trail, with Psalm 33, he is shaping us. Reproving and correcting us. Training us in righteousness that we may be complete, thoroughly equipped for every good work. He is merciful and gracious, slow to anger and abounding in steadfast love and faithfulness. He sees exactly where we are. He knows precisely what we need.

The LORD looks down from heaven;
he sees all the children of man;
from where he sits enthroned he looks out
on all the inhabitants of the earth,
he who fashions the hearts of them all
and observes all their deeds. (33.13–15)

For those who insist on blazing their own trail, stubbornly resisting his counsel and correction, that can be a terrifying thought. But for those who simply want to walk in the light, as he is in the light...

Behold, the eye of the LORD is on those who fear him,
on those who hope in his steadfast love. (33.18)

Sometimes the way is hard. Rocky. Steep. Sometimes we're not sure where he is leading us, or why the path has turned in such a difficult direction. But we believe that our God is good and does good. Therefore...

Our soul waits for the LORD;
he is our help and our shield.
For our heart is glad in him,
because we trust in his holy name. (33.20–21)

And that comforting thought inspires us to pray.

Let your steadfast love, O LORD, be upon us,
    even as we hope in you. (33.22)

I don't know about you, but I needed that walk today. Thanks for traveling the Psalm 33 trail with me.

MONDAY

The Craftsman Whose Work Outlived Moses (and Joshua, and Samuel, and David)

I'm guessing you don't remember his name. You might not have ever even *heard* his name. If I asked you to list the Top-5 Influencers whose work most significantly impacted God's people in the Old Testament, you wouldn't mention him in the same breath as Abraham, Moses, David, or Elijah. I have a strong suspicion we could expand it to the Top-10, Top-25, Top-50 Influencers, and his name still wouldn't come up.

He was just a craftsman, after all. He didn't part the waters of the Red Sea, single-handedly slay a Philistine giant, or call down fire from heaven in a showdown with hundreds of false prophets. He was just a craftsman who lived in the days of Moses, more than 3,000 years ago. But his skillful work outlived Moses, and Joshua, and the judges, and Samuel, and King David.

His name was Bezalel the son of Uri, son of Hur, of the tribe of Judah. The LORD told Moses in Exodus 31:

> ...I have filled [Bezalel] with the Spirit of God, with ability and intelligence, with knowledge and all craftsmanship, to devise artistic designs, to work in gold, silver, and bronze, in cutting stones for setting, and in carving wood, to work in every craft. (31.2–5)

His finished work is so succinctly described in Exodus 37 and 38 that for most, it's quickly glanced at and easily overlooked.

Could I encourage you today to slow down long enough to see and appreciate what's been recorded there for all time:

Bezalel made the ark... (37.1)

The ark of the covenant.

He also made the table... (37.10)

He also made the lampstand... (37.17)

He made the altar of incense... (37.25)

He made the altar of burnt offering... (38.1)

The altar that would sit in front of the tabernacle as *the* place of sacrifice to God... for **centuries**. Generations later, when young Solomon was taking his first steps as Israel's third king, he assembled Israel at Gibeon, before the tent of meeting of God.

> Moreover, the bronze altar that Bezalel the son of Uri, son of Hur, had made, was there before the tabernacle of the LORD. And Solomon and the assembly sought it out. And Solomon went up there to the bronze altar before the LORD, which was at the tent of meeting, and offered a thousand burnt offerings on it. (2 Chron 1.5–6)

That night was *the* life-changing night for Solomon and the history-shaping night for Israel when God appeared and said to the inexperienced king, "Ask what I shall give you." What an incredible invitation! What an amazing night! A night that followed a day that centered around an old altar that had been carried around for centuries. The altar built by a craftsman named Bezalel.

> Bezalel the son of Uri, son of Hur, of the tribe of Judah, made all that the LORD commanded Moses... (Exo 38.22)

...and his work has impacted God's people for millennia. We don't know how long he lived or when he died or how he died or where he was buried. But how many priests faithfully served while using his handiwork? How many souls were comforted as sacrifices for sins were offered on what he built? How many fearful hearts took courage as the ark he constructed was carried before them in battle? How many children's Bible classes around the world have been shown artists' depictions of his work?

And how thankful we ought to be for the men and women whose ability and intelligence, with knowledge, artistic design, and craftsmanship continue to impact God's people. The brother who built the pulpit from which thousands of sermons will be preached. The sister whose colorful bulletin boards shape an entire generation of children in a church family. The designer and maintainer of a website in southern Indiana that will help a seeker in India. A warm meal lovingly prepared for a family that's struggling just to make it through another day.

May we never take for granted what God can do with "just a craftsman."

TUESDAY

The Greatness of Lowliness

At that time the disciples came to Jesus, saying, "Who is the greatest in the kingdom of heaven?" And calling to him a child, he put him in the midst of them… (Matt 18.1–2)

Take a moment to put yourself in the sandals of that child. We don't his name, how old he was, or where he was from. Had his parents been following Jesus for a while? Had he ever seen Jesus perform a miracle? Ever interacted with Jesus before? We don't know. All we know is, on this day, Jesus' disciples had a question. "Who is the greatest in the kingdom of heaven?" And before Jesus gave them an answer, he locked eyes with a child.

I'm guessing that child was shocked when Jesus called him and put him "in the midst" of those disciples. Was he embarrassed? Hesitant? We're not told. But what would *he* have known about *himself* as he looked around at all of those adults? Maybe he was too young to be very self-aware, but not the adults. What would have been readily evident to *them* as *they* looked at that child?

He wasn't the strongest in the crowd. The fishermen who had made their living on the Sea of Galilee were definitely stronger than him.

He wasn't the smartest in the crowd. A tax collector would have needed to be much more savvy than a child to make his way in the Roman Empire.

He wasn't the most experienced in the crowd. Most everybody looking at him would have been more places, seen more things, and accomplished more with their lives.

He wasn't the most eloquent person in the crowd. He didn't wield the most power, hold the most wealth, or carry the biggest reputation. He was just a child. But when the disciples came to Jesus with a question—"Who is the greatest in the kingdom of heaven?"—the Master Teacher called that child to the forefront and drew all adult attention to the most unlikely focal point.

> "Truly, I say to you, unless you turn and become like children, you will never enter the kingdom of heaven. Whoever humbles himself like this child is the greatest in the kingdom of heaven." (18.3–4)

Listen carefully to the kingdom's King. Real greatness isn't defined by muscle, physical prowess, or external beauty. The greatness that truly matters isn't acquired with money or inherited with social status. Kingdom greatness doesn't fly in tandem with cultural accolades, sizable reputations, or big megaphones that amplify even bigger egos. The kingdom of heaven is different. Greater. Eternally significant. Not of this world.

"Truly, I say to you, unless you **turn**…" So says the King. As adults, we become far too easily enamored by the ways the kingdoms of this world measure and celebrate greatness. Meanwhile, the King is calling us to turn. Stop thinking of greatness in terms of physical strength, mental IQ, outward beauty, biggest reputation, loudest mouth, most eloquent tongue, or largest following. Learn and remember that when Jesus gave the definitive answer to the "greatness" question, he didn't call a politician, scholar, model, orator, influencer, best-selling author, millionaire, or the most physically imposing specimen into the midst of the crowd.

He called a child.

Then he called the adults to turn. Become like children. Humble yourselves like that child. Stop measuring greatness like the foolish, shortsighted world. Stop chasing greatness like those with minds set on vain, earthly things.

Allow the King to redefine the terms. Turn and follow him in the greatness of lowliness.

Otherwise, you will never enter the kingdom of heaven.

WEDNESDAY

Be Careful With "I'm the Only One"

"I'm the only one…" The only one who cares. The only one who is really invested. The only one walking by faith. The only one making sacrifices.

Have you ever felt that way? If so, could I encourage you to be careful with "I'm the only one"?

In 1 Kings 19, Elijah the prophet was convinced that he was the last one. Twice he tells God…

> "I have been very jealous for the LORD, the God of hosts. For the people of Israel have forsaken your covenant, thrown down your altars, and killed your prophets with the sword, and I, even I only, am left, and they seek my life, to take it away."

God's answer? "I have seven thousand in Israel who have not bowed the knee to Baal." Elijah was *far* from the only one.

One of the most encouraging things I've learned in working with Christians? I'm only aware of a few of the threads of the enormous good that is being done all around the world by sincere disciples of Jesus. In my little sphere of experience, I'm barely touching the hem of the garment that God is weaving. Even within the life of a single church family, most of us are only aware of a tiny fraction of the good being done day-in and day-out by dedicated saints.

Do we realize that even in this digital age of hyper-sharing where so much attention can be so easily drawn to ourselves, there are men and women of all ages who aren't practicing their righteousness in order to be seen by other people? Every day, all around us …

… sacrifices are made, kindness is shown, prayers are offered, hands are held, tears are shed, comfort is extended, hospitals and funeral homes and prisons are visited, the gospel is shared, prodigals are encouraged, temptation is defeated, real lives are impacted for the better …

… and no trumpet is sounded. No social media post is made. No photo is shared. But the Father who sees in secret knows and is proud.

Let's be careful with "I'm the only one." It wasn't true in Elijah's day. And an untold number of godly people are serving in ways that only heaven knows today. It won't be highlighted on any website or international news segment. It's not out there garnering tens of thousands of comments and shares. But their reward in heaven is going to be great. Yours can be too.

You're not the only one.

THURSDAY

Don't Give the One Who's Looking for "an Opportune Time" an Opportunity

And Jesus, full of the Holy Spirit, returned from the Jordan and was led by the Spirit in the wilderness for forty days, being tempted by the devil. (Luke 4.1–2)

Jesus withstood these temptations, repeatedly returning to "It is written."

And when the devil had ended every temptation, he departed from him **until an opportune time**. (4.13)

The devil departed, but only until another opportunity arose. Years later, Christians would be encouraged by the apostle Peter:

Be sober-minded; be watchful. **Your** adversary the devil prowls around like a roaring lion, seeking someone to devour. (1 Pet 5.8)

The devil continues to prowl, looking **for an opportune time**.

The apostle Paul calls for all of us to be on the alert, humbly aware of our personal vulnerabilities:

Be angry and do not sin; do not let the sun go down on your anger, and **give no opportunity** to the devil. (Eph 4.26–27)

What an important warning that I need to keep at the forefront of my mind:

- When I pick up my smartphone...
- As I move my wrist to click an Internet link...
- As I think about what to search...
- When I'm itching to weigh in on social media...
- When I'm frustrated because I didn't get my way...
- When I'm angry...
- As I'm looking for a diversion from my frustrations...
- When I feel a pull in the direction of bitterness...
- As I'm packing my bags to head out of town...
- When I'm tempted to cheat...
- When it would be advantageous to lie...
- When the darkness is offering a place to hide...

...my Father in heaven has warned me: **give no opportunity** to the one who's seeking "an opportune time" to devour you.

I can't keep the lion from prowling, but I *can* refuse to give him an opportunity. My Lord withstood the temptations of this adversary. Today, he's calling me to be strong in the strength that he supplies.

FRIDAY

God's Answer to the Darkness

Reading Isaiah 8 can feel a little like scanning today's headlines. Conspiracy theories. Fear. Disappointing leaders. False messengers. Misleading "comforters." Distress. Rage. Contempt for authority. Disregard for God. Darkness. Anguish. It's all right there in Isaiah 8, and has been for 2,700 years. It's not a pleasant chapter to read. But the darkness of Isaiah 8 is what helps us see how much we need the light of Isaiah 9, and how precious that light is.

> The people who walked in darkness
>   have seen a great light;
> those who dwelt in a land of deep darkness,
>   on them has light shone. (9.2)

Sound familiar? Seven centuries after Isaiah wrote them, those words were picked up by Matthew and used as a timeless pointer.

> And leaving Nazareth [Jesus] went and lived in Capernaum by the sea, in the territory of Zebulun and Naphtali, so that what was spoken by the prophet Isaiah might be fulfilled:
>
> > "...the people dwelling in darkness
> >   have seen a great light..." (Matt 4.13–16)

Into a world plagued by conspiracy theories, fear, disappointing leaders, false messengers, misleading "comforters," distress, rage, contempt for authority, disregard for God, darkness, and anguish, light began to shine.

For to us a child is born,
    to us a son is given;
and the government shall be upon his shoulder,
    and his name shall be called
Wonderful Counselor, Mighty God,
    Everlasting Father, Prince of Peace.

He's right there in Isaiah 9.

"In him was life," John tells us from the outset of his gospel, "and the life was the light of men. The light shines in the darkness, and the darkness has not overcome it" (John 1.4–5).

Two thousand years later, the light continues to shine. His kingdom stands. The gates of hell shall not prevail against him. Those dwelling in deep darkness still have the opportunity to turn. Listen to him as Counselor. Recognize him as Prince. Follow him into the paths of peace. Submit to him as God.

"The people who walked in darkness have seen a great light…" For 2,700 years the answer—*God's* answer to the darkness of Isaiah 8—has been shining in Isaiah 9.

SATURDAY

Spent For Your Souls

The apostle Paul is beginning to draw his second letter to the Corinthians to a close.

> Here for the third time I am ready to come to you. And I will not be a burden, for I seek not what is yours but you. For children are not obligated to save up for their parents, but parents for their children. I will most gladly spend and be spent for your souls. (2 Cor 12.14–15)

Do you want to make a difference that doesn't cost a dime today? Take a moment to pray for those who are "spent."

- The preachers who have prepared all week to pour out their hearts behind a pulpit tomorrow
- The shepherds who willfully waded into worlds of pain and brokenness this week
- The deacons whose work was indispensable but largely unnoticed last weekend
- The Bible class teachers who gave everything they had to give around a little table with toddlers on Wednesday night
- The people who won't sit with their families in tomorrow's assembly because they will be serving in some other capacity or place

Why? They love the Lord, his people, and the lost. They've already mentally moved on to the next responsibility. Many of them are working full-time secular jobs today. They'll go home tonight and begin preparing for the *next* opportunity. Why? They are willing to most gladly spend and be spent for the souls of others. They love the gospel. They do everything they can to keep the "gospel chariot" rolling along, but they sometimes feel like it ran right over *them* in the process.

Do you want to make a difference that doesn't cost a dime today? Take a moment to pray for those who are gladly spending themselves for the sake of souls. Your soul. "Refresh their hearts" (Philemon 20) by taking the time to express appreciation for their eternity-shaping efforts. And then give a bit of thought to what you might do to help them carry the load.

WEEK NINE

SUNDAY

The Awesome in the Ordinary

By awesome deeds you answer us with righteousness,
O God of our salvation... (Psa 65.5)

If you're like me, it's easy to read a verse like that and think, "Well, I know God's people in ages *past* saw the Lord answer by awesome deeds. The ten plagues on Egypt. The parting of the Red Sea. Water flowing from a desert rock. Manna from heaven. He's a God of awesome *past* deeds for sure, but I've never seen anything like that, so there's a pretty big disconnect between me and David's point in Psalm 65." If you're tempted to think like that (as I have in the past), could I encourage you to slow down and really listen to the message of Psalm 65 today?

By awesome deeds you answer us with righteousness,
O God of our salvation...

...and what sort of "awesome deeds" does David actually go on to describe?

This God established the mountains by his strength (65.6).

Our God stills the roaring of the seas and their waves (65.7).

My God makes the going out of the morning and the evening to shout for joy (65.8).

Your God visits the earth and waters it, softening it with showers and blessing its growth (65.9–10).

This God provides the grain, crowning the year with a bountiful harvest (65.9, 11).

Our God makes the pastures of the wilderness overflow and the green hills to sing with blossoming joy (65.12).

My God clothes the meadows with flocks (65.13).

Your God decks the valleys with grain (65.13).

No, I've never seen the water of a river turn to blood or a sea parted. You've never seen water flow from a rock or manna fall from heaven. And neither had David. But when he looked at mountains, he saw the might of the LORD. When I stand with my feet in the ocean, I'm a witness to my Creator's magnitude. As you watch the sun rise in the morning and set in the evening, you're beholding the joyful work of a glorious Designer and Upholder.

We are surrounded by the awesome of the "ordinary."

And today is another opportunity in a long string of opportunities you've already been given to open your eyes and ears. Behold. Listen. Pay attention. Reflect. See the world around you through the lens of Psalm 65. The Lord of heaven and earth is making, visiting, watering, softening, growing, providing, clothing, showering, decking, crowning, and blessing. Today. He reigns as the hope of all the ends of the earth and of the farthest seas (65.5). And he cares deeply. For you. Just listen…

> O you who hear prayer,
> > to you shall all flesh come.
> When iniquities prevail against me,
> > you atone for our transgressions. (65.2–3)

The establisher of mountains hears your prayers. The Lord of harvests atones for our transgressions. When iniquities prevail against me, he knows. He cares. He has intervened. He invites. He extends and empowers. He saves. Praise is due to this God of our salvation (65.1).

By "awesome deeds"—morning by morning, day after day, evening by evening, night after night—he answers us with righteousness. Sunrises. Spring rains. Green pastures. Summer crops. Flowering meadows. Autumn harvests. Roaring waterfalls. Winter snows. Sunsets. Starlit night skies. "Awesome deeds."

Don't fail to see the awesome in the ordinary today.

MONDAY

The Great Potential of a Tender Heart

He lived during a dark time in Judah's history. His father, King Amon, "did what was evil in the sight of the Lord" and "did not humble himself before the Lord," but "incurred guilt more and more" (2 Chron 33.22–23). Amon was eventually assassinated by his own servants and Josiah—the royal heir—was crowned at the age of eight. It's not hard to imagine how things could have spiraled further out of control, and fast.

But at the age of sixteen, Josiah "began to seek the God of David his father" (34.3). At twenty, "he began to purge Judah and Jerusalem of the high places, the Asherim, and the carved and the metal images."

When Josiah was twenty-six, his secretary told him, "Hilkiah the priest has given me a book." The Book of the Law of the Lord given through Moses had been found in Jerusalem's dilapidated temple. And Shaphan the secretary read from it before the king.

> And when the king heard the words of the Law, he tore his clothes. And the king commanded Hilkiah, Ahikam the son of Shaphan, Abdon the son of Micah, Shaphan the secretary, and Asaiah the king's servant, saying, "Go, inquire of the Lord for me and for those who are left in Israel and in Judah, concerning the words of the book that has been found. For great is the wrath of the Lord that is poured out on us, because our fathers have not kept the word of the Lord, to do according to all that is written in this book." (34.19–21)

Josiah had already shown himself to be a better man than his father and so many of the former kings in his family tree. Now, he was experiencing firsthand the living and active word of God, "sharper than any two-edged sword, piercing to the division of soul and of spirit, of joints and of marrow, and discerning the thoughts and intentions of the heart" (Heb 4.12). The word was being read to Josiah and Josiah was being read by the word. And what was revealed? Not pride. No excuses. Not defensiveness. No blame-shifting. Josiah was revealed to have a tender heart. Just listen to the words a prophetess was instructed to share with the king of Judah:

> "Regarding the words that you have heard, because your heart was tender and you humbled yourself before God when you heard his words against this place and its inhabitants, and you have humbled yourself before me and have torn your clothes and wept before me, I also have heard you, declares the LORD." (34.26–27)

When Josiah heard God's words, his toes were stepped on and he ran as fast as he could **towards** God with a tender heart. No pride. No excuses. No blame-shifting, just an eager, receptive, tender heart. He humbled himself before his Creator. He was ready, willing, and determined to make any change necessary, whatever the cost. And the LORD's response? "Because you heard me, I also have heard you."

Centuries later, things really aren't all that much more complicated, are they? We heard God's words yesterday. Are our hearts tender and humble today? Eager to follow? Ready to apply? Prepared to shine? Looking to make a difference for the good of others and the glory of our King?

> And the king stood in his place and made a covenant before the LORD, to walk after the LORD and to keep his commandments and his testimonies and his statutes, with all his heart and all his soul, to perform the words of the covenant that were written in this book. (34.31)

He heard. He wept. He humbled himself. He learned. He applied. He took a stand. He made a covenant to walk and to keep with all his heart and all his soul. Despite the bad examples before him, this young king led in a different direction and his people followed into a season of great revival. "All his days they did not turn away from following the Lord, the God of their fathers" (34.33).

I'm not a king and you don't live in ancient Judah, but centuries later, things really aren't all that much more complicated. We heard God's words yesterday. The word was read to us and we continue to be read by the word. What is being revealed? Are we humble? Are we learning? Will we keep listening with receptive hearts today and tomorrow? Are we applying? Will we take a stand? Have we made a covenant with the King? Are we walking with him, keeping his commandments with all of our hearts and all of our souls? What impact will we have on the people around us this week? Will our examples be living signs that point to the King or detours in service of the devil?

"Because you heard me, I also have heard you." If we'll show ourselves humble and bold enough to follow in the footsteps of young Josiah, the God of Josiah has promised to hear and lead us as well.

TUESDAY

Opinions: Handle With Care

Opinions. Everybody has them and most of us think ours are better than the next guy's. But as Christians, we need to handle opinions—our own and others'—with care. Listen to the encouragement of Romans 14.1:

> As for the one who is weak in faith, welcome him, but not to quarrel over opinions.

One person believes… while the other person… and what happens next?

The Holy Spirit inspired and preserved this warning for a reason. Opinion-quarrels are common. Opinion-quarrels come easy. Opinion-quarrels can feel exhilarating in the moment, especially when we're looking at pixels instead of pupils. Someone posts an opinion I vehemently disagree with, my provoked spirit is given "full vent" (Prov 29.11), and my fingers fuel-up for the fight. Comments begin to fly faster than I can read or process them, the audience grows, the attention expands… but where does the opinion-quarrel lead? What good comes as a result of my joining the fray?

If I'm not careful, an ugly door in my heart begins to open. I find it incredibly easy within to "despise" a brother or sister in Christ (14.3a). It increasingly feels "right" to "pass judgment" on my fellow disciple (14.3b), "one for whom Christ died" (14.15). And easily forgotten in the opinion-tussle? A fundamental question.

"Who are you to pass judgment on the servant of another" (14.4)? If the Lord has "welcomed" (14.3), is "upholding," and making that brother or sister "stand" (14.4), who am I—simply a fellow, unworthy servant of the same Lord—to pick or escalate a fight over a matter of judgment?

Opinion-skirmishes can exhilarate to the point of intoxication and addiction. Again, there's a reason the apostle Paul warned young Timothy about those who have "an unhealthy craving for controversy and for quarrels about words" (1 Tim 6.4). Think about that. Some have built a deadly appetite for controversy. They've amassed large audiences and built broad platforms with the decaying planks of past feuds. And when they delightfully throw a barrel of fresh fuel on an opinion-fire, attention is quickly drawn, spirits begin to flare, the comments section dissolves into chaos … and what sort of toxic cloud begins to billow who knows where? The rest of 1 Timothy 6.4–5 gives us a pretty good idea…

…envy, dissension, slander, evil suspicions, and constant friction among people who are depraved in mind and deprived of the truth…

Meanwhile, an unbelieving world is watching. The young and weak in faith are listening. And who is rejoicing? Whose domain is allowed to feel a little more real in such moments?

Romans 14 is a powerful reminder: together, we belong to a kingdom that is all about righteousness and peace and joy in the Holy Spirit (14.17). Take a moment to meditate on those words. **Righteousness. Peace. Joy.** How much more eternally significant are those bedrock blessings than my flimsy opinions and fickle personal preferences?

Sometimes, the wisest way to handle opinions is to restrain my words (Prov 17.27–28) and quietly hold back my spirit (Prov 29.11), especially if the quarrel has nothing to do with me. Quarrels get clicks all day, every day, but "whoever meddles in a quarrel not his own is like one who takes a passing dog by the ears" (Prov 26.17).

I am one of many, a single member of a body, called to "look not only to my own interests, but also to the interests of others" (Phil 2.4). When truly compelled to share my opinion, challenge someone else's, or to outright disagree altogether, I would do well to remember, "None of us lives to himself, and none of us dies to himself" (Rom 14.7). Pupils before pixels is probably a pretty good rule of thumb for disagreements in the digital age.

In the end, each one of us will give an account of himself to God (Rom 14.12). Clearly, included in the accounting will be how we handled our own opinions and the opinions of others. So could I suggest Romans 14.20 as a God-breathed nugget worth carrying in your pocket and, most of all, in your heart today? "Do not, for the sake of food, destroy the work of God." Slightly adapted: "Do not, for the sake of (insert matter of opinion here), destroy the work of God." In person and online, "let us pursue what makes for peace and for mutual upbuilding" (Rom 14.19).

Our King expects it and our blood-bought brethren are worth it.

WEDNESDAY

Who's the Real Troubler?

When Ahab saw Elijah, Ahab said to him, "Is it you, you troubler of Israel?" And he answered, "I have not troubled Israel, but you have, and your father's house, because you have abandoned the commandments of the LORD and follow the Baals." (1 Kings 18.17–18)

Live with the Bible as your guide in the twenty-first century and you may be described as a "troubler" of modern culture.

- Jesus as the exclusive path to salvation? **"Intolerant."**
- A faith once for all delivered to the saints? **"Old-fashioned."**
- One body, one Spirit, one hope, one Lord, one faith, one baptism, one God? **"Narrow-minded."**
- The church as pillar and support of the truth? **"Obsolete."**
- God as sovereign over all, including sexuality and marriage? **"Bigoted."**
- Righteousness, self-control, and the coming judgment? **"Unloving."**

Sincerely attempt to keep in step with the Spirit, and some may view you as the "troubler." But 1 Kings 18 reminds us that we aren't the first to be accused of standing on the "wrong side" of history. It also reminds us *why* Elijah believed what he believed, said what he said, and did what he did.

"As the LORD of hosts lives, before whom I stand, I will surely show myself to [Ahab] today." (1 Kings 18.15)

Every single human being on the planet is accountable to the Creator; it's just that some of us submit to that fact, and some of us don't. If the current submitters are described as the "troublers," it's not the first time and it won't be the last.

Let's continue to speak the truth in love. It's what the world needs most. Let's be unashamed of the gospel. It's the power of God for salvation. Let's humbly shine as lights in this dark world. After all, wasn't it Jesus who taught that someone may see our good works and come to give glory to our Father who is in heaven?

Like Elijah, we stand before the LORD of hosts today. The solid Rock. All other ground is sinking sand. To point that out isn't to make trouble. It's to offer hope.

THURSDAY

Mindful of God

Servants, be subject to your masters with all respect, not only to the good and gentle but also to the unjust. For this is a gracious thing, when, mindful of God, one endures sorrows while suffering unjustly. (1 Pet 2.18–19)

How could the apostle Peter possibly encourage servants to treat unjust masters "with all respect"? That's a tough question revolving around an even tougher situation, but the answer isn't tough to find.

…when, mindful of God…

I'm not a servant and you're not a master, but what difference could it make if we looked at today through that same "mindful of God" lens?

- I'm going into this meeting, mindful of God
- I'm engaging in this crucial conversation, mindful of God
- I'm eating lunch, mindful of God
- I'm prioritizing my calendar, mindful of God
- I'm enduring through heartache, mindful of God
- I'm handling frustrations, mindful of God
- I'm offering encouragement, mindful of God
- I'm processing criticism, mindful of God
- I'm traveling on business, away from my family, mindful of God

- I'm seeking to be a peacemaker, mindful of God
- I'm sitting in traffic, mindful of God
- I'm opening the door of my house after an exhausting day of work, mindful of God

It is a humble thing, "when, mindful of God," we count others as more significant than ourselves. It is a gentle thing, "when, mindful of God," we continue to serve even though our service is unappreciated. It is a gracious thing, "when, mindful of God," we treat others, even the unjust, the way we would like to be treated.

"Mindful of God" reminds us of how unworthy we are.

"Mindful of God" helps us stay sensitive to how much we've been forgiven.

"Mindful of God" keeps us desperate for ongoing grace.

"Mindful of God" leaves the outcome in better hands than our own.

"Mindful of God" is a choice.

What impact might it have on your life and the lives of others if you made that choice today?

FRIDAY

"Can I Not Do With You as This Potter Has Done?"

The word that came to Jeremiah from the LORD: "Arise, and go down to the potter's house, and there I will let you hear my words." So I went down to the potter's house, and there he was working at his wheel. And the vessel he was making of clay was spoiled in the potter's hand… (Jer 18.1-4a)

The entire nation of Israel in Jeremiah's day could be compared to this "spoiled" lump of clay—full of potential in the right hands, now marred, misshaped, distorted, and warped.

As hard as it is to look in the mirror sometimes, maybe those ugly words describe your own life—your perspective on the present, your hope for the future, your marriage, the atmosphere of your home, your relationship with God. Marred, misshapen, distorted, and warped. But listen…

…he reworked [the clay] into another vessel, as it seemed good to the potter to do.

Then the word of the LORD came to me: "O house of Israel, can I not do with you as this potter has done? declares the LORD. Behold, like the clay in the potter's hand, so are you in my hand, O house of Israel." (Jer 18.4b-6)

This isn't a question of his presence, desire, or ability. Your misshaped mess is no match for the reforming skill of the Potter. The question for Israel then and the question for us today is this: has everything—*everything*—been surrendered to his will? My public and private life? My perspective? My hope and joy? My marriage? My home? My integrity? My priorities? He can rework *anything* for my good and his glory if I will soften my will and allow him to shape it all "as it seems good to him to do."

So I invite you to think about his question throughout the day. "Can I not do with you as this potter has done?"

Then pray as Jesus taught us to pray, "Your will be done, on earth as it is in heaven" (Matt 6.10).

SATURDAY

The Heart Behind the Hardest Rebukes

It's hard to imagine being one of the original recipients of Paul's first letter to the Corinthians. A letter addressed to you, from an apostle of Jesus, is full of stinging rebukes and challenging admonitions. It would have been humbling; at times, even humiliating. It's what these Christians needed to hear—a tool used by God to put people in their neglected or forgotten place—but it would have been ***hard*** to hear.

Notice, before he issues a single reproof, appeal, or correction, Paul reminds these disciples of the basics—who they are, whose they are, what they can (and should) be through the gospel:

- Called by a faithful God into the fellowship of his Son (1.9)
- Sanctified in Christ (1.2)
- Expected to be saints together with all who submit to the lordship of Jesus (1.2)
- Recipients of grace (1.4)
- Enriched through Christ in all speech and knowledge (1.5)
- Not lacking in any gift (1.7)
- Waiting for the revealing of the Lord (1.7)
- Sustained by the strength of Jesus to the end (1.8)
- Guiltless by the grace of God (1.8)

The Bible isn't an arbitrary rulebook. It's the means God uses to lead us to Christ Jesus, "who became to us wisdom from God, righteousness and sanctification and redemption" (1 Cor 1.30). The "word of the cross" is "the power of God" to save "those who are perishing" (1 Cor 1.18).

And so, when we are willing to follow Paul's lead and "consider our calling" (1 Cor 1.26), we are reminded of the basics—who we are, whose we are, what we can (and should) be through the gospel.

Why, then, would we quarrel with and divide from our fellow believers? Why would we arrogantly tolerate immorality inside the church? Why would we use gifts from God to draw attention to ourselves? Why would we waste our opportunities or live as if our Lord is not faithful to fulfill the promise of his coming?

"Consider your calling, brothers and sisters." Even the sharpest, most difficult-to-read corrections have a context. God reproves, rebukes, and exhorts us because he loves us. If we are going to maintain sensitivity to his corrections, we would do well to consistently consider our calling. If we remember who and whose we are, we'll trust the heart behind the hardest rebukes.

WEEK TEN

SUNDAY

Don't Starve Yourself on the Crumbs of Anxious Toil

When I live as if I am the builder and watchman of my own existence, I'll slowly starve myself to death on "the bread of anxious toil."

I'll be "anxious" because I've convinced myself that my life, my purpose, my happiness revolves around and depends upon me—my willpower, my wisdom, my diligence, my strength.

"Toil"—continuous, exhausting effort—is the perfect word to describe what it will take to construct and maintain the façade that somehow I'm up to the task.

I might be able to convince myself and others for a little while that I am the adequate Definer of my identity, the Maker of my purpose, the Conqueror of all obstacles, the Captain of my happiness, and the Savior of my story, but I won't be able to sustain myself forever on the breadcrumbs of such "anxious toil." Eventually, façades crumble, illusions fail, and masks fall off when we try to fill roles we were never created to play.

But, if I will submit to the LORD as Architect and Builder of the house of my life, the psalmist's words can become my own…

You are good and do good;
   teach me your statutes. (Psa 119.68)

Give me understanding, that I may keep your law
   and observe it with my whole heart. (119.34)

Incline my heart to your testimonies,
    and not to selfish gain! (119.36)

...if I will depend upon the LORD as Watchman of my heart and my hope...

With my whole heart I seek you;
    let me not wander from your commandments! (119.10)

Turn my eyes from looking at worthless things;
    and give me life in your ways. (119.37)

This is my comfort in my affliction,
    that your promise gives me life. (119.50)

...that's life, the way it was meant to be.

How staggeringly, profoundly amazing that the perfectly-wise, all-powerful, ever-present, one and only God would love ... me. That if I will submit to his will and follow his lead, I can confidently live, move, have my being, and ultimately rest in his gracious promises.

Doubt any of that? Just listen to Psalm 127.1–2:

Unless the LORD builds the house,
    those who build it labor in vain.
Unless the LORD watches over the city,
    the watchman stays awake in vain.
It is vain that you rise up early
    and go late to rest,
eating the bread of anxious toil;
    for he gives to his beloved sleep.

Don't starve yourself on the crumbs of self-centered, anxious toil when you've been invited to feast at the table of the King of the universe.

MONDAY

When Our Faces Are Harder Than Rock

O LORD, do not your eyes look for truth?
You have struck them down,
>   but they felt no anguish;
you have consumed them,
>   but they refused to take correction.
They have made their faces harder than rock;
>   they have refused to repent. (Jer 5.3)

How "soft" is your "face" today?
When we're guilty of sin, God wants us to feel anguish, for our own good. In the absence of anguish, we continue to aimlessly wander farther and farther away from the Source of life. Left to our own devices, we will stumble and stagger all the way to eternal separation from him.

And so he straightforwardly tells us in his revelation to mankind that he is willing to strike us down. He is able to consume us. And he does so, at varying times and in differing ways to get our attention, before it is eternally too late.

> God is treating you as sons. For what son is there whom his father does not discipline? If you are left without discipline, in which all have participated, then you are illegitimate children and not sons. Besides this, we have had earthly fathers who disciplined us and we respected them. Shall we not much more be subject to the Father of spirits and live? (Heb 12.7–9)

Reproof and discipline are God-ordained gifts for our good, but like Abraham's descendants of old, we can "refuse to take correction." We can make our faces "harder than rock." We can "refuse to repent."

Here's the fundamental question: is the benefit worth the cost?

Is being hardheaded with your spouse getting you anywhere? Is ignoring the constructive criticism doing you any good? Is the resentment you feel at the one who cared enough to correct really worth it? Is turning your back on the truth leading to happiness with a clear conscience? Is forsaking the ranks of the redeemed for the shadows of the Serpent as fulfilling as was originally promised? Will it last?

Life has a curious way of unraveling when we ignore the will of the Giver of life and refuse to acknowledge our need for him. As long as my life lasts, I have the opportunity to soften my face in repentance. To say, "I'm sorry." To admit that I'm at fault. To acknowledge that there's no one to blame but myself. To penitently come back to my heavenly Father on his gracious terms. Most of us need to soften our faces far more often than we actually do.

Take a long look in the mirror today. Is your face harder than rock because your heart has been hardened by sin? What good is on the horizon if you refuse to repent?

TUESDAY

When the Foundations Are Shaken

Three different groups of people are "shaken" in Acts 16.

One group of men owned "a slave girl" possessed by "a spirit of divination" who brought her owners "much gain by fortune-telling" (16.16). When the apostle Paul commanded the spirit to come out of her in the name of Jesus Christ, "it came out that very hour." What wonderful news for that girl! But her owners? Their hope was shaken. This meddler had come to town and messed up everything! They couldn't care less about the well-being of the girl, all they knew was "their hope of gain was gone" (16.19), and it made them furious. Paul and Silas were dragged before the authorities, beaten with rods, and arrested.

When the foundations are shaken, what we're hoping for and in really matters. For these men, hope was gone.

One group of men spent the next few hours in prison. Paul and Silas had brought the gospel of King Jesus to the Roman colony of Philippi. They'd spent time along a river at a place of prayer, sharing the good news with a group of women. Lydia and her household had been baptized. What wonderful news! Now, Paul and Silas were in the city's inner prison with their feet fastened in stocks. "Many blows" had been inflicted upon them. It was midnight after a rough day. But *their* hope *wasn't* gone. "Paul and Silas were praying and singing hymns to God, and the prisoners were listening to them" (16.25).

When the foundations are shaken, what we're hoping for and in really matters. For these men, hope was alive and well.

One man almost took his life that night.

> Suddenly there was a great earthquake, so that the foundations of the prison were shaken. And immediately all the doors were opened, and everyone's bonds were unfastened. When the jailer woke and saw that the prison doors were open, he drew his sword and was about to kill himself, supposing that the prisoners had escaped. But Paul cried with a loud voice, "Do not harm yourself, for we are all here." And the jailer called for lights and rushed in, and trembling with fear he fell down before Paul and Silas. (16.26–29)

When the foundations are shaken, what we're hoping for and in really matters. For this man, hope was no longer in an earthly empire or social status or job security. For this man, hope was hanging by the thread of the most important question of all.

> "Sirs, what must I do to be saved?" And they said, "Believe in the Lord Jesus, and you will be saved, you and your household." And they spoke the word of the Lord to him and to all who were in his house. And he took them the same hour of the night and washed their wounds; and he was baptized at once, he and all his family. Then he brought them up into his house and set food before them. And he rejoiced along with his entire household that he had believed in God. (16.30–34)

Three different groups were "shaken" in Acts 16.

One group got angry. Their hope was gone, so they resorted to violence.

One group was steadfast. Their hope was alive, so they prayed and sang hymns to God from prison at midnight.

One man was desperate. His only hope was the Lord Jesus, so he was baptized at once and rejoiced with his entire household as a new day dawned.

When the foundations are shaken, what we're hoping for and in really matters.

WEDNESDAY

Don't Skip Chapter 1

Nehemiah was a descendant of Abraham. A thousand miles away from home. In the backwash of Israel's exile. Somehow, he had come to serve as cupbearer to Artaxerxes, king of the mighty Persian Empire. And Nehemiah had just heard heartbreaking news.

> "The remnant there in the province who had survived the exile is in great trouble and shame. The wall of Jerusalem is broken down, and its gates are destroyed by fire." As soon as I heard these words... (Neh 1.3-4a)

What comes to mind when you think of Nehemiah? If you're familiar with the story contained in the book of the Bible that bears his name, I'm guessing you think of the rebuilding of Jerusalem's walls. After all, fifty-two days? That's an incredible feat, especially when we remember the intense opposition he and his people faced. And the work involved so much more than rebuilding the walls. Sacred observances had to be reestablished. Sins had to be confessed. The covenant had to be revisited. Reforms upon reforms. Through it all, Nehemiah proves to be an admirable leader, modeling principles that continue to be talked about centuries later. But before it all is this first chapter.

As soon as I heard these words...

What did Nehemiah do? As cupbearer to the king, he has access to the most powerful man on the planet. His heart's desire is to go home, back to Jerusalem. Maybe he can have an impact?

Perhaps he can do some good. What's the plan? Where does it start? When can we get to it? It's time to get busy. Spring into action. Get things done.

Could I encourage you to slow down long enough to notice what may be the most easily overlooked (and indispensable?) "leadership lesson" of all?

> As soon as I heard these words I sat down and wept and mourned for days…

Nehemiah allowed himself time to feel.

> …and I continued fasting and praying before the God of heaven.

Nehemiah knew who was needed more than anyone. Higher help than Artaxerxes. Greater wisdom than any scribe. Infinitely more important than himself and his own ideas.

> And I said, "O Lord God of heaven…"

This is who you have revealed yourself to be.

> "…the great and awesome God who keeps covenant and steadfast love with those who love him and keep his commandments…"

I'm asking you to hear me.

> "…let your ear be attentive and your eyes open, to hear the prayer of your servant that I now pray before you day and night for the people of Israel your servants…"

I and my people are unworthy of your attention, compassion, and intervention.

> "…confessing the sins of the people of Israel, which we have sinned against you. Even I and my father's house have sinned. We have acted very corruptly against you and have not kept the commandments, the statutes, and the rules that you commanded your servant Moses."

But I'm humbly asking you to remember your promises. They are all I have to cling to. All I have to build upon.

> "Remember the word that you commanded your servant Moses, saying, 'If you are unfaithful, I will scatter you among the peoples, but if you return to me and keep my commandments and do them, though your outcasts are in the uttermost parts of heaven, from there I will gather them and bring them to the place that I have chosen, to make my name dwell there.'"

You are our Redeemer. Our gracious Savior in the past. Our only hope in the present.

> "They are your servants and your people, whom you have redeemed by your great power and by your strong hand."

I believe you can change this heartbreaking, uncertain, frightening situation, and I am willing to play my part in whatever ways you are willing to use me.

> "O Lord, let your ear be attentive to the prayer of your servant, and to the prayer of your servants who delight to fear your name…"

Please, be with me as I have a crucial conversation with the most powerful person I have ever known.

> "…give success to your servant today, and grant him mercy in the sight of this man."

Nehemiah knew his people needed more than Nehemiah. Nehemiah believed the God of heaven would be more critical to his success than the King of earth. And that's the reason. Before an articulate appeal. Before travel plans. Before wall blueprints. Before a stirring speech in Jerusalem. Before the logistics. Before the reforms. Before it all, Nehemiah took the time to feel, to grieve, and to pray. Without it, I'm guessing we wouldn't have Nehemiah 2–13.

Which makes me wonder. What chapters of potential, perspective, and power fail to get written in our own lives because we arrogantly, shortsightedly skip Chapter 1?

> As soon as I heard these words I sat down and wept and mourned for days, and I continued fasting and praying before the God of heaven.

THURSDAY

Jesus Knew

John was there and he wants to make sure we understand. Jesus knew.

> Now before the Feast of the Passover, when **Jesus knew** that his hour had come to depart out of this world… (John 13.1)

Jesus knew what was about to happen. We hear him telling his mother in John 2, "My hour has not yet come." Throughout John's Gospel, we are reminded on several occasions that certain things happened or didn't happen "because his hour had not yet come." But in John 13, Jesus knew. Tomorrow would be the most difficult day of his life. If ever there was a time to *be* served, now was that time.

> **Jesus, knowing** that the Father had given all things into his hands, and that he had come from God and was going back to God… (13.3)

Jesus knew who he was. I AM. Fulfillment of prophecy. Light and hope of the world. The way, the truth, and the life. The door. The good shepherd. Israel's true King. Imminent conqueror of death. On his way back to the Father's right hand.

Jesus knew. And perfectly equipped with that knowledge, what did he do? He rose from supper…

> He laid aside his outer garments, and taking a towel, tied it around his waist. Then he poured water into a basin and began to

wash the disciples' feet and to wipe them with the towel that was wrapped around him. (13.4–5)

Divinely aware of everything, Jesus assumed the role of the lowliest servant. He knew that Simon Peter would deny him three times before daybreak (13.38), and he washed those dirty feet anyway.

Jesus knew how Judas would spend the rest of that night…

"You are clean, but not every one of you." For **he knew** who was to betray him… (13.11)

…and he washed those filthy feet anyway.

Jesus knew.

Sometimes, I think *I* know. After all, I'm fully aware of *my* needs, *my* wants, the things *I* deserve, who *I* am, *my* status, what *I've* earned, where *I'm* headed, and if only you knew what I know about myself, you'd realize that *I'm* the one who ought to be catered to. I'm the one who deserves the first and the best. Ever felt that way? "Don't you know who I am?" "Don't you know what I have on my plate?" "Don't you know what I have to put up with?" Far too easily and often, what we think we know about ourselves entices and empowers us to believe that lowly things like self-denial, sacrifice, and service are beneath us.

And then we're reminded in John 13 of what Jesus knew. In fact, that's the basis of Paul's encouragement to all Christians in Philippians 2.5–7:

Have this mind among yourselves, which is yours in Christ Jesus, who, though he was in the form of God, did not count equality with God a thing to be grasped, but emptied himself, by taking the form of a servant…

Jesus knew what tomorrow held. Jesus knew who he was. Jesus knew the denial and betrayal before it happened. And knowing it all, he chose to serve anyway.

"Have this mind among yourselves." Five challenging words to remember today.

FRIDAY

What Does Holiness Look Like?

In Leviticus 19, "the LORD spoke to Moses, saying, 'Speak to all the congregation of the people of Israel and say to them, **"You shall be holy, for I the LORD your God am holy"** (19.1). Like columns throughout the chapter, he punctuates every few verses with **"I am the LORD your God."**

Maybe you're not sure what God means by "holiness." *Leviticus* isn't the most widely read book in our Bibles, but take a look at just how practically our Creator speaks throughout the nineteenth chapter...

- Revere your mother and father (19.3)
- Don't turn to idols (19.4)
- Offer your sacrifices in the way I've told you (19.5–8)
- Provide for the poor and the sojourner (19.9–10)
- Don't steal (19.11)
- Don't deal falsely (19.11)
- Don't lie to one another (19.11)
- Don't profane my name (19.11)
- Don't oppress your neighbor or rob him (19.13)
- Give the hired worker what you owe (19.13)
- Don't curse the deaf or put a stumbling block before the blind (19.14)
- Judge in righteousness, avoiding partiality (19.15)
- Don't go around as a slanderer (19.16)

- Don't hate your brother in your heart (19.17)
- Don't take vengeance or bear a grudge (19.18)
- Love your neighbor as yourself (19.18)

"You shall be holy, for I the LORD your God am holy." This is what the Creator told the descendants of Abraham. This is how he reasons with Christians.

> As obedient children, do not be conformed to the passions of your former ignorance, but as he who called you is holy, you also be holy in all your conduct, since it is written, "You shall be holy, for I am holy." (1 Pet 1.14–16)

Holiness isn't some sort of an abstract idea that lacks real-life application. Take a long look at that list from Leviticus 19. That's the way we ought to live this week, isn't it? Why? **"I am the LORD your God."**

SATURDAY

The Ripple Effects of Me on Me

Imagine with me for a moment…

It's Sunday. Yesterday, I invited a neighbor to church. This morning—Sunday morning—she walked through the doors with her family and I couldn't be more excited (maybe a little nervous) for her to sit with me. It all goes great, her kids loved their Bible classes, and she says they'll be back next Sunday. Fantastic!

It's Monday morning, the next day. We become social media friends. As new social media friends sometimes do, she scrolls through my profile posts and shares. Eventually, she reaches five months ago in my timeline. She remembers, that was a hard month for a whole lot of people. There was a storm of concerning, confusing, scary, divisive things swirling around in the world, and everybody had an opinion about it. Sometimes, the expressing of those opinions turned ugly. Really, really ugly.

Having sat beside me in church yesterday, what will she discover about how I handled that tough season as a disciple of Jesus? How will the things I said five months ago sound today? Will what she sees on my social media profile deepen her respect for what she saw in church yesterday and make her even more anxious to discover the reasons behind my faith, hope, and love? Or will there be strange, conflicting differences between "in person" me of this weekend and "social media" me from five months ago?

Or, put another way, will the influence for Christ I hope to have five months from now be strengthened or weakened by what I'm saying and how I'm saying it today?

"You are the light of the world." (Matt 5.14)

We who are strong have an obligation to bear with the failings of the weak, and not to please ourselves. Let each of us please his neighbor for his good, to build him up. (Rom 15.1–2)

The whole law is fulfilled in one word: "You shall love your neighbor as yourself." But if you bite and devour one another, watch out that you are not consumed by one another. (Gal 5.14–15)

Do nothing from selfish ambition or conceit, but in humility count others more significant than yourselves. Let each of you look not only to his own interests, but also to the interests of others. (Phil 2.3–4)

Walk in wisdom toward outsiders… Let your speech always be gracious, seasoned with salt… (Col 4.5–6)

I would do well to remember the ripple effects I can all too easily have, not only on me and my neighbor, but the reputation of Jesus Christ and his church.

WEEK ELEVEN

SUNDAY

The Light That Guides the Upright through the Darkest Situations

Psalm 140 is a difficult psalm to read. It's not full of complicated words, but it *is* full of difficult people and dark situations. Throughout the psalm, we get to listen in as David pours his heart out to God.

> Deliver me, O LORD, from evil men;
>> preserve me from violent men,
> who plan evil things in their heart
>> and stir up wars continually.
> They make their tongue sharp as a serpent's,
>> and under their lips is the venom of asps.
> Guard me, O LORD, from the hands of the wicked;
>> preserve me from violent men,
>> who have planned to trip up my feet.
> The arrogant have hidden a trap for me,
>> and with cords they have spread a net;
>> beside the way they have set snares for me. (140.1–5)

What can you pray at such a difficult time? On what should you set your hope? Where is the light in the midst of such darkness?

I'm thankful that the LORD led David through the shadows of that season to the last verse of Psalm 140. I'm thankful for his preserving these last words as an enduring light for three millennia:

Surely the righteous shall give thanks to your name;
the upright shall dwell in your presence. (140.13)

People *choose* to be upright. *I* can choose to be upright, and so can you. I can't control what other people do, but I *can* make the choice to be a person of patience, kindness, and integrity. You can't control how other people treat you, but you *can* resolve to travel the path of treating others the way you would like to be treated. We can't control what other people say, but we *can* "surely" choose to "give thanks" to our Father's name, trusting that he sees. He knows. He cares.

Psalm 140.13 is an ancient signpost, plainly pointing in a direction labeled **UPRIGHTNESS**. It's not a crowded path and it's mostly uphill. The shadows are sometimes deep and the people we encounter can be really, really hurtful. But the signpost stands, bearing this message: "The upright shall dwell in God's presence."

A thousand years after David wrote those words, his greatest heir would sit on the side of a mountain and preach, "Blessed are the pure in heart, for they shall see God" (Matt 5.8). Seeing God. It's the greatest desire of the upright heart. More than retaliation. More than revenge. It's the choice that the upright make. "More than anything else, I want to see God and dwell in his presence." This is the way of the upright.

If we'll take the time to look, this ray of light continues to shine from our Father's throne, leading us home, even in the darkest of situations. Let's give thanks to his name today.

MONDAY

In My Hand No Price I Bring

In Genesis 43, Jacob and his sons find themselves between the proverbial rock and a hard place. Severe famine has enveloped the earth. Of the ten sons who had gone to Egypt to buy grain, only nine had returned. The last time they had seen their brother Simeon, he was being bound before their eyes. To top it all off, on their way home, the nine had found their money that should have been left in exchange for Pharaoh's grain in the mouth of their sacks. "At this their hearts failed them, and they turned trembling to one another" (Gen 42.28).

When father Jacob and his family had eaten the grain the sons had brought from Egypt, scared hearts began to give way to hungry stomachs. Jacob is understandably wary of losing any more sons, but something has to give.

> Then their father Israel said to them, "If it must be so, then do this: take some of the choice fruits of the land in your bags, and carry a present down to the man, a little balm and a little honey, gum, myrrh, pistachio nuts, and almonds. Take double the money with you. Carry back with you the money that was returned in the mouth of your sacks." (43.11–12)

Even at a time of severe famine, Jacob knows that his sons cannot present themselves empty-handed before an authoritative figure who wields the power of life and death. If his sons must go, they will go with the best of what the family can scrape together. Perhaps these paltry gifts will soften the heart of Pharaoh's governor.

We also live in an age of famine, severe thirst, great trial, and death. Ours is a famine of righteousness, thirst for meaning, trials of our own making, and separation from the Giver of life. At a time when our own hearts ought to feel the weight of failure and our spirits should be trembling, far too many of us continue to practice ungodliness and cheer on those who do the same.

But self-centered hearts on a godless trajectory have a way of hitting rock bottom. Like the prodigal son of Luke 15, we squander everything that matters most in reckless living. And when we've spent it all, we experience firsthand the desperation of famine, the bitterness of severe thirst, the consequences of our decisions, the absence of life, light, and peace.

Do we dare come before the King of the universe in such a state? We are absolutely unworthy. His wrath is rightfully revealed from heaven against all ungodliness and unrighteousness of men who have been suppressing the truth. We are guilty. Separated from Christ. Strangers to the covenants of promise. Without hope. Without God. What could we possibly scrape together from the pit of our famished souls to soften the heart of this King?

Just then, we hear his voice.

> The Spirit and the Bride say, "Come." And let the one who hears say, "Come." And let the one who is thirsty come; let the one who desires take the water of life without price. (Rev 22.17)

Water of life. Without price.

This King isn't asking for the choice fruits of your land. There is no present you can put together as sufficient for a bribe. "Double the money" means nothing to him.

What *is* he looking for? Bankruptcy of spirit. Mourning over sin. Meekness. Hunger and thirst for righteousness. Spirits melted by mercy and ready to share mercy with others. Purity in heart. Peacemakers. Those who are willing even to be persecuted for righteousness' sake.

> Could my tears forever flow,
>> Could my zeal no languor know,
> These for sin could not atone;
>> Thou must save, and Thou alone.
> In my hand no price I bring,
>> Simply to Thy cross I cling.

Augustus M. Toplady (1776)

TUESDAY

To Abide In or Go On Ahead?

Watch yourselves, so that you may not lose what we have worked for, but may win a full reward. Everyone who goes on ahead and does not abide in the teaching of Christ, does not have God. Whoever abides in the teaching has both the Father and the Son. (2 John 8–9)

DO NOT ENTER. NO TRESPASSING. STAY ON THE TRAIL.

We recognize warnings to respect existing boundaries. We see them all the time.

WRONG WAY. ROAD CLOSED AHEAD. DO NOT TOUCH.

In 2 John 9, we're being warned by our Creator to respect an eternally-significant boundary. The "Holy and Righteous One," the very "Author of life" (Acts 3.14–15), has revealed "the way, the truth, and the life" (John 14.6). If we love him, we will keep his commandments (John 14.15). Without him, outside of him, apart from him, there is no way to our heavenly Father.

But our Creator has also blessed us with free will. Day by day, we have choices: In what will I seek satisfaction? Who is my master? On what will I set my heart?

Each of us will make a fundamental choice today: will I abide in the teaching of Christ, or "go on ahead"? My "Leader and Savior" (Acts 5.31) offered himself that I—a self-proclaimed enemy of God—might find grace to "abide" *in* and *with* the perfectly holy Creator of the universe. But he has also warned me, because he loves me, of the dangers outside the boundaries of his will.

> "Abide in me, and I in you. As the branch cannot bear fruit by itself, unless it abides in the vine, neither can you, unless you abide in me. I am the vine; you are the branches. Whoever abides in me and I in him, he it is that bears much fruit, for apart from me you can do nothing." (John 15.4–5)

Abide in or go on ahead: this is the fundamental choice, and it is a choice with consequences. To go on ahead is to go without God. To abide in the teaching of Christ is to be brought under his authority and into harmony with the Father.

To abide in or go on ahead? How will I handle that choice today?

WEDNESDAY

Not One Word Did (or Will) Fail

The last three verses of Joshua 21 form one of the great summary statements in all the Old Testament.

> Thus the LORD gave to Israel all the land that he swore to give to their fathers. And they took possession of it, and they settled there. And the LORD gave them rest on every side just as he had sworn to their fathers. Not one of all their enemies had withstood them, for the LORD had given all their enemies into their hands. Not one word of all the good promises that the LORD had made to the house of Israel had failed; all came to pass. (Josh 21.43–45)

Land, rest, and **victory**—each was a testament to the faithfulness of God. Not one word of all his good promises had failed. From this point forward, Israel could look back and recognize, "all came to pass."

But these ancient summary statements have also been preserved for *our* learning and they ought to continue to shape *our* perspective. We serve the same faithful God. For now, we sing the anthem written by Samuel Stennett in 1787…

> We will rest in the fair and happy land,
> Just across on the evergreen shore,
> Sing the song of Moses and the Lamb,
> And dwell with Jesus evermore.

With faith in the promises of God, we sing and pray and reflect on what we *will* do "by and by." But just as surely as Israel could look back in the days of Joshua and appreciate what the LORD *had* done, so one day will we also look back at the fulfillment of glorious promises and prophecies. Can you imagine?

"The coming of the Lord *has* happened."

"Jesus *did* bring with him those who *had* fallen asleep."

"The Lord himself *did* descend from heaven with a cry of command."

"All who were in the tombs *did* hear his voice and come out."

"Those who were alive *were* caught up together with them in the clouds and they *did* meet the Lord in the air."

"And so we *are* and will always be with the Lord."

"Not one word of all the good promises that God made to his people has failed; all *has* come to pass."

Why read Old Testament books of the Bible like Joshua?

For whatever was written in former days was written for our instruction, that through endurance and through the encouragement of the Scriptures we might have hope. (Rom 15.4)

In the meantime, we patiently wait, building our faith in the God who always keep his promises.

THURSDAY

God, a Two-Year-Old, and a Terrifying Lawnmower

When our youngest daughter Emma was two years old, she was terrified—absolutely, positively *terrified* of lawnmowers. She didn't want to be outside if I was mowing. She didn't want to be within sight of a lawnmower. She didn't even like the sound of a running lawnmower from somewhere else in the neighborhood.

I remember one Summer day when all three of our girls were playing in the backyard. Sunshine. Warm weather. A Slip 'n Slide. All seemed right with the world... until I came around the corner with the lawnmower. Emma immediately screamed, waddled into the house, and refused to reemerge until the lawnmower was back in the garage. I just shook my head and went on with my monotonous mowing. Honestly, I was more than a little frustrated.

But as I mowed line after line of grass on that hot Summer day, I tried to put myself in her tiny shoes. The handle of the lawnmower was taller than Emma. Its roar was probably the loudest noise she'd heard to that point in her life. And here's the key—she had no idea that I was the guiding force behind the mower. In her 2-year-old mind (as far as I could tell), the lawnmower had a mind of its own. It was unpredictable. Dangerous. At that age, she hadn't learned that the mower moved only when her father made it move.

Aren't we the same way as adults? How frequently we forget that in the darkest, scariest, most threatening moments of life, we—our circumstances, well-being, and ultimate outcome—are under the guiding hand of our heavenly Father!

> Count it all joy, my brothers, when you meet trials of various kinds, for you know that the testing of your faith produces steadfastness. And let steadfastness have its full effect, that you may be perfect and complete, lacking in nothing. (James 1.2–4)

Temptations are everywhere. They are strong, alluring, and hard to resist. But listen to God's book:

> No temptation has overtaken you that is not common to man. God is faithful, and he will not let you be tempted beyond your ability, but with the temptation he will also provide the way of escape, that you may be able to endure it. (1 Cor 10.13)

Cancer. Hurricanes. Persecution. Floods. Divorce. Famine. Miscarriages. Are they daunting? Yes. Can they lead to despair? Most certainly. But in the grand scheme of the universe, are they comparable to runaway lawnmowers? Is God desperately trying to accomplish his purposes while heartlessly neglecting his children? Hardly.

> We know that for those who love God all things work together for good, for those who are called according to his purpose. (Rom 8.28)

There is a loving, guiding, wise, powerful influence greater than anything else in this world and beyond. Yes, life under the sun comes with terrible hardships and unspeakable heartaches. But our Father reigns supreme. Not one tear falls that he does not notice (Psa 56.8). And when we remember that truth and anchor ourselves to it, there is nothing that can separate us from his love.

> Who shall separate us from the love of Christ? Shall tribulation, or distress, or persecution, or famine, or nakedness, or danger, or sword? As it is written, "For your sake we are being killed all the day long; we are regarded as sheep to be slaughtered." No, in all these things we are more than conquerors through him who loved

us. For I am sure that neither death nor life, nor angels nor rulers, nor things present nor things to come, nor powers, nor height nor depth, nor anything else in all creation, will be able to separate us from the love of God in Christ Jesus our Lord. (Rom 8.35–39)

Even death is subject to his will. It will mow each one of us down, but even death serves his purposes and will be abolished when he determines. For God's child, informed and emboldened with God's perspective, death will have no victory and very little sting in the light of eternal life (1 Cor 15.53–57).

The day came when Emma figured out that the lawnmower only moves under the guiding hand of her father. The mower still roars, but she's realized that there isn't any real reason to be afraid. She's grown to trust the watchful eye and tender care of her father, even when things are a little scary.

I hope to live and die with that sort of perspective as well.

FRIDAY

You Should Remember

Elijah. Elisha. Amos. Jonah. Joel. Hosea. Micah. Isaiah. Zephaniah. Habakkuk. Jeremiah.

Over the course of nearly 300 years, the LORD called, rebuked, and warned his people through "the prophets." **Three hundred years.** Think about that. The United States hasn't been around that long. For a longer stretch than we have been a nation, God sent prophets to Israel and Judah. With that in mind…

> In [Jehoiakim's] days, Nebuchadnezzar king of Babylon came up, and Jehoiakim became his servant for three years. Then he turned and rebelled against him. And the LORD sent against him bands of the Chaldeans and bands of the Syrians and bands of the Moabites and bands of the Ammonites, and sent them against Judah to destroy it, **according to the word of the LORD that he spoke by his servants the prophets.** (2 Kings 24.1–2)

The back third of the Old Testament can be a challenging section of Scripture. Why is it worth the effort? Among many other things, it teaches and reminds us that **God always keeps his word.** Nebuchadnezzar rose up and Judah was destroyed "according to the word of the LORD that he spoke by his servants the prophets."

Does that really matter thousands of years later on the other side of the world? It matters more than most can possibly imagine.

> **…you should remember the predictions of the holy prophets** and the commandment of the Lord and Savior through your

apostles, knowing this first of all, that scoffers will come in the last days with scoffing, following their own sinful desires. They will say, "Where is the promise of his coming? For ever since the fathers fell asleep, all things are continuing as they were from the beginning of creation." For they deliberately overlook this fact, that the heavens existed long ago, and the earth was formed out of water and through water by the word of God, and that by means of these the world that then existed was deluged with water and perished. But by the same word the heavens and earth that now exist are stored up for fire, being kept until the day of judgment and destruction of the ungodly.

But do not overlook this one fact, beloved, that with the Lord one day is as a thousand years, and a thousand years as one day. The Lord is not slow to fulfill his promise as some count slowness, but is patient toward you, not wishing that any should perish, but that all should reach repentance. **But the day of the Lord will come**... (2 Pet 3.2-10a)

Jerusalem was destroyed by Nebuchadnezzar more than 2,600 years ago. From God's perspective, it might as well have been last Saturday.

For three centuries prior to that destruction, kings and beggars doubted the warnings, ignored the rebukes, and rejected the calls. But God kept his word.

God *always* keeps his word.

"By the same word the heavens and earth that now exist are stored up for fire, being kept until the day of judgment and destruction of the ungodly." Even on a Friday in the twenty-first century, we should remember the predictions of the holy prophets.

SATURDAY

The Body You'll Need

If one member suffers, all suffer together... (1 Cor 12.26)

I've spent a lot of time in funeral homes in recent months. It's been a heavy season as many I know and love have lost spouses, parents, grandparents, and children. There have been lots of tears. Lots of hugs. Lots of hard days and long nights.

But not one of these people I know and love has suffered alone. They are members of the body of Christ, and that fact has made an incalculable difference as they walk these dark valleys.

> For just as the body is one and has many members, and all the members of the body, though many, are one body, so it is with Christ. For in one Spirit we were all baptized into one body—Jews or Greeks, slaves or free—and all were made to drink of one Spirit. For the body does not consist of one member but of many. (1 Cor 12.12–14)

If the entire body were a thumb and that thumb gets smashed by a hammer, the body is going to be in sad shape. If the entire body were an arm and that arm gets broken, how will the body function? If the entire body were a foot and that foot can't bear any weight, how will the body press on? "If all were a single member, where would the body be?" (12.19). Good question.

> But God has so composed the body, giving greater honor to the part that lacked it, that there may be no division in the body, but

that the members may have the same care for one another. If one member suffers, all suffer together; if one member is honored, all rejoice together. Now you are the body of Christ and individually members of it. (12.24–27)

It's a beautiful, humbling, inspiring thing when you see God's plan lived out by ordinary people. Just within the past few weeks...

I've had a brother in Christ recovering from open heart surgery ask me from his hospital bed how a fellow brother in a battle with cancer is doing.

I've seen armies of sisters in Christ provide and serve more food than a grieving family (and all their extended family) could eat in a week.

I've seen a brother in Christ drive more than a thousand miles to surprise and comfort his grieving brother in Christ at the funeral home.

I've seen teenage Christians rallied and organized to clean the house of a grieving family before their out-of-town relatives arrive.

I've seen brethren open their homes for as long as is needed.

I've seen anonymous givers cover extraordinary costs.

I've heard disciples sing *Amazing Grace* and *Where the Roses Never Fade* and *It Is Well With My Soul* as the grieving family on the front row couldn't muster a syllable, but were helped to feel the hope and conviction flowing from those hymns.

In every single funeral home I've been in during this heavy season, I've heard some Christian say, "I don't know how people without a church family go through days like today."

If one member suffers, all suffer together...

That's not ever really on our minds when we spend an hour after an assembly of worship just talking and laughing and getting to know each other in the foyer or the parking lot, is it? We're not thinking about future suffering when we meet for early-morning coffee, or a teen devo, or a small group study, or Friday night pizza-

and-a-movie with families from church. A future gathering at the funeral home isn't on our radar when we meet the family who just moved to the area in their new driveway and help them unload the U-Haul. When we host a baby shower, or attend a middle school musical, or show up to cheer on the high school senior at his last football game, future grief is almost inconceivable. But these are the times—over the course of months and years and decades—when ordinary people become "fellow members" who will be there, in the darkest times of life, to lift drooping hands, strengthen weak knees, and suffer together.

When the funeral home seems a million miles away, don't take the small, ordinary, everyday relationship-building opportunities around you and your family for granted. Even then, God is composing his body. It's a body you'll need when the days are hard and the nights are long.

WEEK TWELVE

SUNDAY

What King Delights in a Doorkeeper?

Who am I—so very small, weak, and shortsighted—that he would even notice me?

> Great is our Lord, and abundant in power;
> his understanding is beyond measure. (Psa 147.5)

Why should he care about me?

> He determines the number of the stars;
> he gives to all of them their names. (147.4)

What meaningful thing could I possibly offer him?

> He covers the heavens with clouds;
> he prepares rain for the earth;
> he makes grass grow on the hills. (147.8)

What could I ever do that would appear as even the tiniest blip on heaven's radar?

> He gives snow like wool;
> he scatters frost like ashes.
> He hurls down his crystals of ice like crumbs;
> who can stand before his cold?
> He sends out his word, and melts them;
> he makes his wind blow and the waters flow. (147.16–18)

To be known by him? Remarkable. To be forgiven by him? Amazing. To be granted the opportunity to serve him for a lifetime? Incredible. Undeserved. Grace.

But to be a source of *delight* to him? What king delights in a doorkeeper? To somehow bring joy to his measureless heart? I'm guessing most of us would find that hard to imagine, so let's just listen together to the way the Lord of the universe is described in Psalm 147.10–11:

> His delight is not in the strength of the horse,
>   nor his pleasure in the legs of a man,
> but the Lord takes pleasure in those who fear him,
>   in those who hope in his steadfast love.

Who are you that he would even notice you? What registers as more than a blip on heaven's radar? Not your looks or the number of your followers or your net worth. The namer of the stars isn't awed by your accomplishments or accolades. He needs absolutely, positively not one thing from you.

And yet, he takes pleasure in those who fear him. He delights in those who joyfully hope in his steadfast love. "Who like me Thy praise should sing, O Almighty King?" Just a lowly, humble hoper, desperately dependent on his loyal love. And that's enough. More than enough, it's what sparks joy in heaven's throne room.

> Praise the Lord!
>   For it is good to sing praises to our God;
>   for it is pleasant, and a song of praise is fitting. (147.1)

What king delights in a doorkeeper? My King.

MONDAY

We Become What We Worship

They went after false idols and became false… (2 Kings 17.15)

Our Creator knew what he was talking about when he warned us about idolatry. We become what we worship. Follow the lead of false "gods" and you will inevitably "become" false.

Worship **money**? Covetousness will take deep root in your heart and greed will become your defining ambition.

Worship **sex**? Those created in the very image of God will become nothing more than objects to be consumed on the altar of your pleasure.

Worship **power**? People will be simply pawns on your personal chessboard.

Worship **violence**? It will be increasingly easy to hate (and hurt) others without cause.

Worship **celebrity**? The artificial, the Photoshopped, and the carefully choreographed will somehow come to mean more to you than the imperfect (but real) flesh-and-blood in your own home.

Worship **self**? For a little while, you'll sit on your homemade throne and live like a tiny tyrant…

…but only for a little while. Why? Because when we "go after" false "gods," we're suppressing the truth (Rom 1.18). We're exchanging the real glory of the immortal God for foolish, false images (Rom 1.23). Claiming to be wise, we will live like fools. Why? Because we become what we worship.

That fact will be terrible news or life-changing good news, depending on the **object** of our worship. In Colossians 1.15, the Lord Jesus Christ is presented as "the image of the invisible God." Colossians 3.10 describes the opportunity to "put on the new self, which is being renewed in knowledge after the image of its creator." Jesus is the true and better image who leads to abundant, eternal life.

We are *all* worshipers. It's simply a matter of who or what we are worshiping. Either way, we will become what we worship.

Worship carefully.

TUESDAY

"Namely Jesus"

Hebrews 2 calls for your close attention. It warns about our tendency to "drift away" from what matters most. And it asks a sobering question: "How shall we escape if we neglect such a great salvation?"

But why? *Why* should I lend my precious attention on a Tuesday to a 2,000-year-old letter? Why should I be concerned about "drifting away" from any*thing* or any*one*? What is this "salvation," and what makes it great?

"Namely Jesus." There's a face attached to this message of salvation. A face with a name. "We see him… namely Jesus…"

- For a little while, Jesus was made lower than the angels (2.9)
- Jesus shared in flesh and blood (2.14)
- Jesus suffered when he was tempted (2.18)
- Jesus tasted death for everyone (2.9)
- Jesus served as the atoning sacrifice for our sins (2.17)
- Jesus became the founder of our salvation (2.10)
- Jesus has been made a merciful and faithful high priest in the service of God on our behalf (2.17)
- Jesus is able to help those who are being tempted (2.18)
- Jesus is the devil-Destroyer and the deliverer of all those who through fear of death were subject to lifelong slavery (2.15)
- Jesus is not ashamed to call those of us who have been sanctified by his sacrifice brothers and sisters (2.11)

"Namely Jesus."

Perhaps you're having the sort of day where David's question from Psalm 22, reiterated in Hebrews 2, is *your* question:

> "What is man, that you are mindful of him,
>   or the son of man, that you care for him?"

The answer to that question has a face and a name—**Jesus**. Jesus knows. Jesus cares. Jesus gave. Jesus sympathizes. Jesus helps. Jesus is interceding. For you.

"How shall we escape if we neglect such a great salvation?"

He's worthy of your attention and submission today.

WEDNESDAY

"You Have Not Passed This Way Before"

Joshua was the newly-appointed leader of God's people. After more than 40 years' worth of wandering in the desert wilderness between Egypt and Canaan, the descendants of Abraham were about to step foot for the first time in the Promised Land. Slavery and the consequences of stubborn rebellion against God stood behind them, war stood before them on the other side of the Jordan River. How could they possibly succeed? How would they know where to go, when to go, and what to do?

> Then Joshua rose early in the morning and they set out from Shittim. And they came to the Jordan, he and all the people of Israel, and lodged there before they passed over. At the end of three days the officers went through the camp and commanded the people, "As soon as you see the ark of the covenant of the Lord your God being carried by the Levitical priests, then you shall set out from your place and follow it. Yet there shall be a distance between you and it, about 2,000 cubits in length. Do not come near it, in order that you may know the way you shall go, for you have not passed this way before." (Josh 3.1–4)

"You have not passed this way before." In at least one important way, that's true of you and me. Today.

This infant nation of Israel was told to follow the ark of the covenant of the Lord their God, "in order that you may know the way you shall go." Why? "For you have not passed this way before."

You and I aren't following a golden box wherever it's carried by a group of Israelite priests throughout the day, but we *have* been blessed with God's complete revelation to mankind and prayer. Thousands of years after Joshua, we've received our own God-given "marching orders."

> In all circumstances take up the shield of faith, with which you can extinguish all the flaming darts of the evil one; and take the helmet of salvation, and the sword of the Spirit, which is the word of God, praying at all times in the Spirit, with all prayer and supplication. To that end, keep alert with all perseverance.... (Eph 6.16–18)

Why? "In order that you may know the way you shall go." What does that have to do with me? Today? "For you have not passed this way before."

When Israel failed to look to the LORD for direction as to where and when and how they ought to go, they encountered disaster. It was a bitter lesson learned over and over and over again. But am I any better off if I approach a new God-given day without deliberately taking up the shield of faith and the helmet of salvation? "I have not passed this way before." Thank God I have been blessed with the sword of the Spirit and the opportunity to pray "at all times." But what am I doing with these God-given resources? Am I learning to use them? Is my skill growing? Am I leaning on them as indispensable to success and life itself?

Who knows what today will bring for any of us? But that is precisely the point. The Lord God Almighty does. He has provided everything we need in order to know the way we ought to go, come what may. **We have not passed this way before.**

Have we taken the time today to hear from the One who has?

THURSDAY

Don't Believe Your Accuser

In Revelation 12, we read about **the accuser**—the great dragon, that ancient serpent, who is called the devil and Satan, the deceiver of the whole world. John hears a loud voice in heaven, saying, "Now the salvation and the power and the kingdom of our God and the authority of his Christ have come, for **the accuser** of our brothers has been thrown down, who **accuses** them day and night before our God" (Rev 12.10).

Accusers charge others with offenses or crimes. Accusers find fault. Accusers blame.

But think about this news. In the middle of this incredible revelation of Jesus Christ, the deceiver of the whole world is thrown down. The one who has accused men and women before God "day and night" for millennia is defeated, "and there was no longer any place" for him in heaven (12.8).

Where this accuser has found fault, the Lamb of God has forgiven. Where he has charged, the Christ has covered. Where the accuser has blamed, the Savior has intervened.

- "He's rebelled." True, but Jesus obeyed in full.
- "She's unrighteous." True, but Jesus is perfectly righteous.
- "I deceived him." True, but Jesus was never deceived.
- "Her sins have made her filthy." True, but Jesus has washed her clean.
- "He's been unholy." True, but Jesus has sanctified him.

- "She's been guilty." True, but Jesus has justified her.
- "He's unworthy." True, but Jesus is willing to welcome him.
- "She wandered far from God." True, but Jesus is not ashamed to call her "sister."

The accuser has been thrown down. The salvation and the power and the kingdom of our God and the authority of his Christ have come. Every single charge the accuser can muster is no match for the blood of the Lamb (12.11). And now…

> There is therefore now no condemnation for those who are in Christ Jesus. (Rom 8.1)

That's where this blessing is enjoyed. "In Christ." If you are in Christ, there is no condemnation, and if there is no condemnation rightly laid at your feet, why would you believe anything this accuser has to say today?

"No condemnation." If God has said it, you can believe it, because your accuser is no match for the blood of your Savior.

FRIDAY

If You Knew the Hail Was Going to Fall Tomorrow

Then the Lord said to Moses, "Rise up early in the morning and present yourself before Pharaoh..." (Exo 9.13)

...so Moses went, armed with the warning of a seventh plague. Water had turned to blood. Frogs, gnats, and flies had filled the land. Livestock had died, boils had broken out in sores on man and beast... but Pharaoh would not yield to let the children of Israel go. And so, yet another warning.

> "Behold, about this time tomorrow I will cause very heavy hail to fall, such as never has been in Egypt from the day it was founded until now. Now therefore send, get your livestock and all that you have in the field into safe shelter, for every man and beast that is in the field and is not brought home will die when the hail falls on them." (9.18–19)

Earlier in the chapter, in warning about the fifth plague:

> The Lord set a time, saying, "Tomorrow the Lord will do this thing in the land." And the next day the Lord did this thing. All the livestock of the Egyptians died, but not one of the livestock of the people of Israel died. (9.5–6)

The Lord set a time. "I will do this thing tomorrow." And the next day, he did the thing.

Now, early in the morning, he's warned that a *seventh* plague is on the horizon. "About this time tomorrow." Think about that. If you knew devastating hail "such as never has been in Egypt" was going to fall tomorrow, what would you do? Listen to the LORD's patience: "Now therefore send, get your livestock and all that you have in the field into safe shelter." He gives them an entire day to prepare!

If you knew the hail was going to fall tomorrow, what would you do today? I love how simply Exodus 9.20–21 frames the two choices:

> Then whoever feared the word of the LORD among the servants of Pharaoh hurried his slaves and his livestock into the houses, but whoever did not pay attention to the word of the LORD left his slaves and his livestock in the field.

Some hurried to act, some didn't pay attention. Simple as that. Those who respected the LORD enough to fearfully listen to his gracious warning did what was necessary to find "safe shelter" from the impending demonstration of his wrath. Those who didn't respect him enough to pay attention to his clear warning went about their lives, doing whatever they wanted, without any preparation. And about that time the next day, "the LORD rained hail upon the land of Egypt" (9.23).

It's one thing to read Exodus 9 and shake your head at the stubbornness of those who failed to heed the warning.

> But do not overlook this one fact, beloved, that with the Lord one day is as a thousand years, and a thousand years as one day. The Lord is not slow to fulfill his promise as some count slowness, but is patient toward you, not wishing that any should perish, but that all should reach repentance. But the day of the Lord will come like a thief, and then the heavens will pass away with a roar, and the heavenly bodies will be burned up and dissolved, and the earth and the works that are done on it will be exposed.
>
> Since all these things are thus to be dissolved, what sort of people ought you to be in lives of holiness and godliness...? (2 Pet 3.8–12)

Moses isn't warning you today that the most devastating hail imaginable is going to fall about this time tomorrow. But the same God who warned Pharaoh through Moses has graciously warned you. "The day of the Lord will come." How patient he has been with us! And some have acted. Some are paying no attention. "Safe shelter" in Jesus is abundantly available to any who respect God enough to fearfully listen to his warnings. Those who don't respect him enough to pay attention will go about their lives in whatever way they choose without any preparation at all.

But do not overlook this one fact. Your Creator has set a time. He has told us, "I will do this thing." And on the day of his choosing, he will do the thing.

If you knew the hail was going to fall tomorrow, what would you have done?

> Therefore, beloved, since you are waiting for these, be diligent to be found by him without spot or blemish, and at peace. (2 Pet 3.14)

SATURDAY

The Tent That Is Your Earthly Home

What's the longest span of time you've spent in a tent? Me? Five days in the Great Smoky Mountains.

I love tents. I love camping. I love the outdoors. But I also love coming back to my house once the tent time is over. Back to hot water, the convenience of a kitchen, a clean bathroom, and a soft bed.

Did you know that the apostle Paul used the idea of a tent to teach some really important truths? He was a tentmaker by trade after all (Acts 18.1–3), and he used this simple, everyday thing that everyone can easily picture to powerfully broaden our perspective. Listen to what he shares in 2 Corinthians 5…

> For we know that if the tent that is our earthly home is destroyed, we have a building from God, a house not made with hands, eternal in the heavens. (5.1)

What is this "tent" that is your "earthly home"?

> For in this tent we groan, longing to put on our heavenly dwelling, if indeed by putting it on we may not be found naked. For while we are still in this tent, we groan, being burdened—not that we would be unclothed, but that we would be further clothed, so that what is mortal may be swallowed up by life. He who has prepared us for this very thing is God, who has given us the Spirit as a guarantee. (5.2–5)

Your "tent" is the part of you that's "mortal." Paul is talking about your body. Slow down and think about that for a moment. *Your* body is just a tent—a fragile, temporary dwelling place. It's your earthly home for now, but it's not eternal. We may diet, exercise, supplement, and subscribe to every gimmick known to man, but our bodies are prone to groan. Life under the sun inevitably takes a toll on each one of our "tents."

And yet, by God's Spirit, Paul is revealing what lies beyond our temporary tent time. We have a building from God, a house not made with hands, eternal in the heavens. What is "mortal" will eventually be "swallowed up" by life. He who has prepared us for this very thing is God, and arming ourselves with his perspective changes everything.

> So we are always of good courage. We know that while we are at home in the body we are away from the Lord… (5.6)

If God has prepared glorious things for me, how would he have *me* prepare? If this "earthly home" is temporary, how can I make the most of my limited time and resources? How can I avoid wasting this precious opportunity? What must I do to inherit that eternal house not made with hands? Let's allow Paul to continue as our inspired guide throughout the rest of the chapter. What more does he have to share?

Walk by faith, not by sight (5.7). Faith comes from listening to and applying what God has said in his word. Live in it. Walk by it. Cling to it.

Live with the determined awareness that it's better to be away from these bodies and at home with the Lord (5.8). Don't put any temporary thing before your eternal Maker.

Make it your ultimate aim to please him (5.9). Every day. Everywhere. In all circumstances. Whatever is going on. The aim is to please the Lord.

Fight to maintain a God-shaped sense of awe. "For we must all appear before the judgment seat of Christ, so that each one may receive what is due for what he has done in the body, whether good or evil" (5.10).

Knowing the fear of the Lord, work to persuade others (5.11). You've come to know the truth. You've been shown what lies beyond. Share it with those who can't yet see because they don't yet know.

As a living sacrifice, give yourself over to the controlling love of Christ. He died for you so that you might no longer live for yourself, but for him who for your sake died and was raised (5.14–15). Reconciliation with God is possible in Christ. For our sake, the Father made his Son—who knew no sin—to be sin, so that in him we might become the righteousness of God (5.21). For what could we possibly live that's more substantial than that?

Train yourself to look at people as so much more than physical bodies (5.16). As C.S. Lewis wrote in *The Weight of Glory*, "There are no ordinary people. You have never talked to a mere mortal. Nations, cultures, arts, civilizations—these are mortal, and their life is to ours as the life of a gnat. But it is immortals whom we joke with, work with, marry, snub and exploit—immortal horrors or everlasting splendors." From now on, therefore, we ought to regard no one simply in terms of their flesh.

If you are in Christ, you are a new creation (5.17). The old has passed away. Even today, our Creator beckons. "Behold. The new has come." A foretaste is already available of what will ultimately be through the Lord who is making all things new.

Tents serve a purpose. They can facilitate great experiences and help us make lasting memories. But sometimes they make us groan and long for something more. If you want to see as your Father in heaven sees today, take little moments here and there to remember. In the car. In line. With your family. In the quiet. Tent time isn't permanent time. We have a building from God. A house not made with hands. Eternal in the heavens.

In the meantime, enjoy the journey. Be of good courage. Live like a pilgrim. Long for home.

WEEK THIRTEEN

SUNDAY

A Simple Lesson From a Child's Cough

Several years ago, our family was looking forward to a February week in Florida for a large lectureship filled with lots of singing, Bible study, and catching up with friends. Like many, we'd battled the common January sniffles, sore throats, and a bit of bronchitis, but by the time we boarded a plane bound for Tampa, our family was pretty much back to 100% healthy. There was just one lingering reminder of January's respiratory challenges—the occasional dry cough of our youngest daughter, Emma.

One night during that busy week, as a crowd of more than a thousand people gathered to sing in a gymnasium, that adventurous 8-year-old convinced us to let her sit with her 10-year-old sister, Jadyn, high above the gymnasium floor on the tip-top row of bleachers. We could always see them, but they were a *long* ways away.

Put that many people together in a confined space during Winter and even when the crowd is "quiet," you'll notice a pretty consistent chorus of sniffles, sneezes, and coughs. But I noticed something that night. In the midst of that large crowd and all the noise that came with it, every time my 8-year-old coughed, I could tell it was her. I recognized the sound of her cough above all others, not because it was the loudest, but because it was *her* cough. The cough of my daughter.

I think about that night when I read Psalm 116.1–2:

I love the LORD, because he has heard
   my voice and my pleas for mercy.
Because he inclined his ear to me…

Do you realize that the LORD can hear and recognize your voice today? You are one on a planet of billions and billions of people, and yet, he hears *your* voice. In fact, he is able and willing to incline his ear to you. Right here, right now. Incredible.

…therefore I will call on him as long as I live.

Today is a great day to put that resolution into practice, to call with our enormous family of brothers and sisters on the Father in heaven who knows and hears each one of us.

I will offer to you the sacrifice of thanksgiving
   and call on the name of the LORD. (116.17)

What a blessing! Happy Lord's day.

MONDAY

Developing the Knee-Jerk Reaction to Pray

Nehemiah was a man of prayer. When he heard that the walls of Jerusalem were broken down and its gates destroyed by fire, he prayed "before the God of heaven." Nehemiah 1 records a lengthy cry to "the great and awesome God who keeps covenant and steadfast love with those who love him and keep his commandments."

But Nehemiah's prayers weren't always long. At times, they seem to have been spur-of-the moment, internal, knee-jerk reactions to what was going on around him. If you had been looking at him in the flesh, you might not have even been able to tell that internally he was approaching the throne of God above in prayer.

> The king said to me, "What are you requesting?" So I prayed to the God of heaven. (2.4)

> When Sanballat heard that we were building the wall, he was angry and greatly enraged, and he jeered at the Jews... Hear, O our God, for we are despised. (4.1, 4)

> I did not demand the food allowance of the governor, because the service was too heavy on this people. Remember for my good, O my God, all that I have done for this people. (5.18–19)

> For they all wanted to frighten us, thinking, "Their hands will drop from the work, and it will not be done." But now, O God, strengthen my hands. (6.9)

Tobiah and Sanballat had hired [Shemaiah] ... that I should be afraid and act in this way and sin, and so they could give me a bad name in order to taunt me. Remember Tobiah and Sanballat, O my God, according to these things that they did... (6.14)

Then I commanded the Levites that they should purify themselves and come and guard the gates, to keep the Sabbath day holy. Remember this also in my favor, O my God, and spare me according to the greatness of your steadfast love. (13.22)

Remember me, O my God, for good. (13.31)

What a great reminder for the day! What a worthy goal for our long-term spiritual health: to practice and develop and nurture the knee-jerk reaction to pray!

Most certainly, there's a time to sit down—as Nehemiah did in chapter 1—to bow your head, close your eyes, and pray at length, perhaps even with tears and fasting. But there are also times, in the heat-of-the moment, to quickly seek the face and favor of the God who hears.

"Help me answer with wisdom."

"Hear, O God, what is being said."

"Remember me, O my God."

"Strengthen me."

"Help."

Surrounded by far too many whose knee-jerk reactions trend toward bitterness, wrath, anger, clamor, slander, malice, and ugly retaliation, we have the opportunity to shine as lights today. Even if the people around you aren't able to tell that your heart—in the blink of an eye—has entered heaven's throne room...

Rejoice always, pray without ceasing, give thanks in all circumstances; for this is the will of God in Christ Jesus for you. (1 Thes 5.16–18)

TUESDAY

A Savior and Friend, Deeply Moved

Illness. Death. Grief. They are some of the hardest experiences in life. What makes them even harder? When it seems as if we're experiencing them alone.

In John 11, a certain man was ill, Lazarus of Bethany. When Jesus hears, he stays two days longer in the place where he was, and Lazarus dies. Upon his arrival, Jesus listens as not one, but two sisters lament, "Lord, if you had been here, my brother would not have died."

Rays of divine glory shine throughout John 11. "I am the resurrection and the life." "Did I not tell you that if you believed you would see the glory of God?" "Lazarus, come out." The claims and accomplishments of Jesus were astounding. But could I focus your attention on a phrase that draws us into the very heart of Jesus?

> When Jesus saw Mary weeping, and the Jews who had come with her also weeping, he was **deeply moved** in his spirit… (11.33)

> Jesus, **deeply moved** again, came to the tomb… (11.38)

Deeply moved. Jesus was deeply moved by a friend's illness. He "loved Martha and her sister and Lazarus" (11.5). Jesus was deeply moved by a loved one passing through the valley of the shadow of death. "Our friend Lazarus has fallen asleep, but I go to awaken him" (11.11). Jesus was deeply moved by the tears of Lazarus' sisters. "Jesus wept" (11.35).

Illness. Death. Grief. They are some of the hardest experiences in life. And when it seems as if we're experiencing them alone, it's even harder. But if John 11 teaches us anything, it's that we're really not alone.

We won't always understand his timing, his plans, or his methods, but we are not alone. Our Savior knows what it is to be deeply moved. I believe he continues to be deeply moved when a sinner repents, a prodigal comes home, a song of praise is sung from the heart, or an act of selfless service is performed in the shadows. I believe the One who called his disciples to weep with those who weep continues to be deeply moved by our grief. We are not alone in our pain.

And even when the time comes for me to walk through the valley of death's shadow, I don't have to be afraid. "For you are with me." My Lord is also my friend, a friend with a heart that has been and continues to be deeply moved.

He still asks, as he asked Martha, "Do you believe this?"

WEDNESDAY

"Like Any Other Man"

In spite of his extraordinary physical strength, Samson was vulnerable, "like any other man."

> After this [Samson] loved a woman in the Valley of Sorek, whose name was Delilah. And the lords of the Philistines came up to her and said to her, "Seduce him, and see where his great strength lies, and by what means we may overpower him, that we may bind him to humble him. And we will each give you 1,100 pieces of silver." So Delilah said to Samson, "Please tell me where your great strength lies, and how you might be bound, that one could subdue you." (Judges 16.4–6)

Notice carefully Samson's increasingly dangerous responses to Delilah's repeated enticements.

> "If they bind me with seven fresh bowstrings that have not been dried, then I shall become weak and be **like any other man**." (16.7)

> "If they bind me with new ropes that have not been used, then I shall become weak and be **like any other man**." (16.11)

> "If you weave the seven locks of my head with the web and fasten it tight with the pin, then I shall become weak and be **like any other man**." (16.13)

> And he told her all his heart, and said to her, "A razor has never come upon my head, for I have been a Nazirite to God from my

mother's womb. If my head is shaved, then my strength will leave me, and I shall become weak and be **like any other man.**" (16.17)

You see, in spite of his extraordinary physical strength, Samson was remarkably "like any other man." How so?

> Can a man carry fire next to his chest
>   and his clothes not be burned?
> Or can one walk on hot coals
>   and his feet not be scorched? (Prov 6.27–28)

"Like any other man."

Whomever you are—man *or* woman—I challenge you to make that personal today. I'm determined to do the same. "I am *not* immune to temptation. I *can* be lured and enticed by my own desire. My own deceitful desires *can* give birth to sin. I *can* fall. I *can* be devoured by the roaring lion. I *can* be lost. Therefore, I *must* be on guard against temptation, **like any other man.**"

Thank God there is good news of great hope.

> No temptation has overtaken you that is not **common to man.** God is faithful, and he will not let you be tempted beyond your ability, but with the temptation he will also provide the way of escape, that you may be able to endure it. (1 Cor 10.13)

How can you be stronger than Samson today?

> Be strong in the Lord and in the strength of his might. Put on the whole armor of God, that you may be able to stand against the schemes of the devil. (Eph 6.10–11)

Only then will you be equipped to fight alongside the King of kings and Lord of lords who was not and is not "like any other man."

THURSDAY

What Will Be Clear After Death

When he opened the fifth seal, I saw under the altar the souls of those who had been slain for the word of God and for the witness they had borne. They cried out with a loud voice, "O Sovereign Lord, holy and true, how long before you will judge and avenge our blood on those who dwell on the earth?" Then they were each given a white robe and told to rest a little longer, until the number of their fellow servants and their brothers should be complete, who were to be killed as they themselves had been. (Rev 6.9–11)

On this side of death, there may be seasons when we struggle to maintain confidence in an all-present, all-powerful, all-knowing God who reigns supreme with perfect power and complete authority.

On this side of death, there are stormy days and dark nights that can strain our feeble grasp on the anchor of a Lord who is beyond reproach in his holiness and love.

On this side of death, there will be heartbreaking moments that shake the very foundations of faith in a King who is true and worthy of our trust.

On this side of death, believers must walk by faith.

But on the other side of death? How different is the story!

On the other side of death, faith is unnecessary. After all, "faith is the assurance of things hoped for, the conviction of things not seen" (Heb 11.1). On the other side of death, we will see.

On the other side of death, there is no reason to hope. "Hope that is seen is not hope. For who hopes for what he sees?" (Rom 8.24). On the other side of death, hope will have been realized.

On the other side of death, the root of the obedience of faith will have borne the fruit of an eternal reward. "Be faithful unto death," says our Savior, "and I will give you the crown of life" (Rev 2.10). On the other side of death, perfectly lit with eternal perspective, the heaviest earthly burdens will seem to have been strangely "light." The longest, darkest, scariest valleys will be recognized as having been so very "momentary." We will realize that even the most difficult afflictions experienced under the sun have ultimately served to prepare for us "an eternal weight of glory beyond all comparison" (2 Cor 4.17). On the other side of death, it will be clear. The weight of our temporary crosses was as nothing when exchanged for the blessed weight of our Christ-given, faith-won crowns.

Revelation 6.9 envisions "the souls of those who had been slain for the word of God and for the witness they had borne." *Slain.* What a terrible, violent word. Faith led them to their deaths. Conviction cost them their lives. But on the other side of death, there is no doubt in their minds. No wavering in their praise. Their dedication may have required the greatest of earthly sacrifices, but their God reigns and they have eternally conquered.

"O Sovereign Lord, holy and true…"

One day, there will be no doubt. Things hoped for will be things enjoyed. Conviction of things not seen will give way to realized satisfaction forever. The challenge today is to trust in what will be abundantly clear then.

For the things that are seen are transient, but the things that are unseen are eternal. (2 Cor 4.18)

FRIDAY

The End?

Do you have any idea what the last two words of the last book of the Old Testament are? It's a far cry from, "And they lived happily ever after." The Old Testament ends with these two sad words: "utter destruction."

Destruction is littered all over the first thirty-nine books of the Bible. There are destroyed cities, walls, and gates. There are a devastating number of destroyed lives, marriages, and families. One of the tragic themes of the Old Testament—especially throughout the prophets—is that the root cause of so much of the "utter destruction" is Israel's unfaithfulness to their covenant with God. By the time we reach Malachi 4—the last chapter of the last book of the Old Testament—a destroyed covenant has led to a destroyed temple and a destroyed kingdom. "Utter destruction." Sad, but fitting.

And yet, just before those last two Old Testament words are written, God inspires his prophet to deliver a beautiful promise:

> But for you who fear my name, the sun of righteousness shall rise with healing in its wings. (Mal 4.2)

"Utter destruction" is a dangerous possibility, but it doesn't have to be where the story ends.

On the flip side, do you have any idea what the last words of the New Testament are? "The grace of the Lord Jesus be with all. Amen." That's a gloriously far cry from "utter destruction."

What's the difference? More accurately, *who's* the difference? The Lord Jesus is the difference, even today.

This morning's sun has risen on "utter destruction" in every direction. Everywhere we look, sin has ravaged lives, marriages, and families. Maybe that hits very personally close to home for you today. If so, there is *such* good news.

"Utter destruction" doesn't have to be the last word of your story. The Son of Righteousness has risen, conquered death, and opened the door to healing from sin for those who fear his name. "The grace of the Lord Jesus" can be where your story takes the turn toward life eternal.

Destruction or grace. How do you want your story to end?

"He who testifies to these things says, 'Surely I am coming soon.' Amen. Come, Lord Jesus!" (Rev 22.20)

SATURDAY

Last Book, Last Page, Last Words

Choosing last words can be quite the challenge. What's the best, most effective and thought-provoking way to wrap up a crucial conversation? A Bible class? An article? A sermon? A book? With what do we want to leave our audience when all is said and done? Many of us struggle on that front.

But the Bible? How could you possibly conclude the written revelation of Almighty God to mankind? With 66 books produced over the span of 1,500 years using dozens of different authors, how do you round off such an incredible masterpiece? I'm pretty sure I'd struggle with that for multiple lifetimes, but God didn't. His Book has a last page with last words. As I read them, a few of those words really stand out.

"The river of the water of life" (22.1). It's described as bright as crystal, flowing from the throne of God and of the Lamb. After a lifetime of wandering past mirages, knowing better, but still sometimes trying to drink the sand and coming away bitterly disappointed yet again, here is life. The water of life. An entire river, flowing, never-ending, sourced by the Giver and Sustainer of life.

"The tree of life" (22.2). What was lost on Page 3 of the Bible is highlighted on its last page. Accessible once again. Thriving. Offered. Enjoyable. Its leaves will be for the healing of the nations. No longer will there be anything accursed to threaten or take advantage of it. In fact, all curses will have been decisively dealt with and banished. Here, sinners who have washed their robes in the blood of the Lamb will "have the right" to the tree of life (22.14). Unhindered. Unobstructed. Unashamed.

"**Worship**" (22.3). The throne of God and of the Lamb will be in the midst of God's people, and they will sing the praises of him who is worthy of blessing and honor and glory and might with voices that never fade or fail.

"**They will see his face**" (22.5). Night will be no more. Shadows will no longer deepen. Tears won't cloud our vision. Death will never close another eye. There will be no mourning, no crying, no pain. Those will be "former things" that have "passed away" (21.4). There will be no need for lamp or sun. God's glorious face, now fully revealed, will provide the light.

"**Forever and ever**" (22.5). No timer. No countdown. No expiration date. No end.

"**These words are trustworthy and true**" (22.6). Their author abounds in steadfast love. They are rooted in the unchangeable character of his eternal purpose. He is not fickle and he cannot lie. He is perfectly, infinitely faithful, and he will surely do what he has promised.

"**Blessed**" (22.7). Infinitely happy and satisfied will be those who trust and obey the God of infinite faithfulness.

"**I am coming soon.**" You see, the last page of the Book isn't the end of the Story. It's finished, but forward-looking. "Behold" (22.7, 12). "Surely" (22.20). The long-awaited King will return. Could it be today?

"**Come**" (22.17). To all who are thirsty and famished, heavy laden and weary, the invitation stands. The Spirit invites. The Bride encourages as the Bridegroom patiently waits a little longer. The path has been blazed, the truth has been revealed, the price has been paid. "Let the one who desires take the water of life without price."

"**I warn**" (22.18). God means what he says. His word is not idle or empty, but living and active, sharper than any two-edged sword.

Nothing—no action or thought or intention of the heart—can be hidden from him. All are exposed to the eyes of him to whom we must give account. My share in the tree of life and the holy city is on the line. Heaven and hell are in the balance. What could I possibly enjoy here for a few days, weeks, months, years, or decades that would be worth the consequences of failing to take his warnings seriously?

"Come, Lord Jesus!" (22.20). This is the cry of a citizen of heaven whose mind is set on things above.

> O God, you are my God; earnestly I seek you;
>> my soul thirsts for you;
> my flesh faints for you,
>> as in a dry and weary land where there is no water. (Psa 63.1)

If his steadfast love really is better than life (Psa 63.3), why wouldn't the deepest cry of my heaven-inclined heart be, "Come"? "I'm ready. I'm eager. Come."

"Grace" (22.21). Of all the ways to conclude, the last page of the last book in the greatest Book ever written ends on this note: Grace is real. Grace is alive. Grace is personal. Grace is available. Grace is abundant. Grace is the way to victory. Sin and Satan and death don't have to have the last word in your story. No, your story, your song for all eternity, can be grace.

The grace of the Lord Jesus be with all. Amen.

May it be so.

THE DAILY SEARCH FOR
WONDROUS THINGS: VOLUME 1

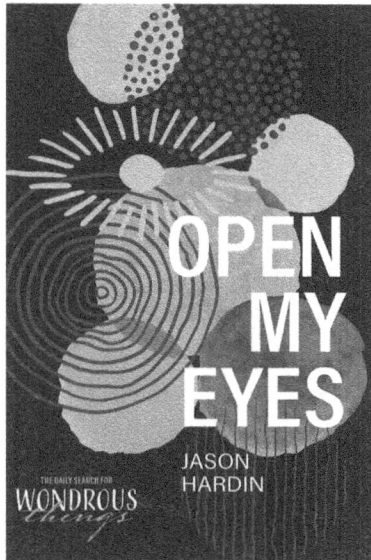

"Open my eyes, that I may behold wondrous things out of your law."
(Ps 119.18)

www.deward.com

ALSO BY JASON HARDIN

Boot Camp
Equipping Men with Integrity for Spiritual Warfare

Jason Hardin has a desire to equip the men of today to live lives of integrity. In his book, *Boot Camp: Equipping Men with Integrity for Spiritual Warfare*, he provides a Basic Training manual in spiritual warfare equipping men to fight for honor, integrity and a God-glorifying life.

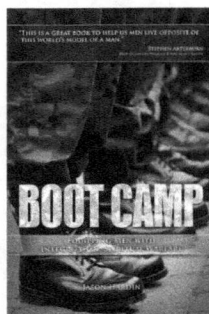

Hard Core
Defeating Sexual Temptation with a Superior Satisfaction

Hard Core deals with how to defeat sexual temptation and find something more satisfying. So many—men *and* women—are being slaughtered in their struggle with sexual sin. Individual lives, marriages, children, influences for good, ministries of gospel preachers, and entire congregations of the Lord's people are being seriously impacted.

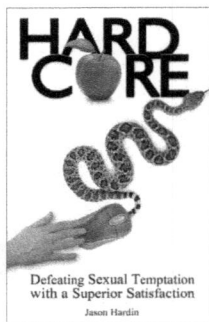

Hello, I'm Your Bible
A Practical Guide to Accurately Handling the Word of Truth

Hello, I'm Your Bible is a practical guide to understanding and applying God's word of truth. Whether you've just been introduced to the Bible, you'd like to get reacquainted with the Scriptures, or you're looking to grow in your ability to help others in their walk of faith, *Hello, I'm Your Bible* can guide you into a deeper relationship with the God behind the living and active word.

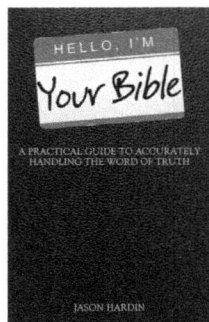

For a full listing of our books, visit DeWard's website:

www.deward.com

www.ingramcontent.com/pod-product-compliance
Lightning Source LLC
LaVergne TN
LVHW041315080426
835513LV00008B/475